Juz One Explained

The Student's Quran

Dr. Muddassir Khan

In the Name of Allah, The Most Merciful,
The Bestower of Mercy.

Introduction

This book is a combination of translation and interpretation. The translation of the words of the Quran and the translation of the interpretation come as one sentence with a common, complete meaning, so that it is easier to read and easier to understand.

Direct approximate translation of the words of the Quran is presented in plain text, and the entire interpretation is in brackets.

The text in square brackets [...] must be read beginning with the words "that is..."

Allah Almighty sent down to people His Book - the Quran, as guidance, distinction, light and mercy. The Quran was sent down to the Prophet Muhammad (peace and blessings of Allah be upon him) who explained to his companions (Allah be pleased with them) the meaning of His verses. Subsequently, these explanations were passed on to the next generations. This is how the science of interpreting the Quran - *tafsir* - arose.

By reading only a direct translation of the words of the Quran, it is impossible to correctly understand the meaning of many verses, therefore the text of the Quran and its interpretation must be linked. At an early stage of learning the Quran, it is better to use simple and short commentaries so that the main meaning of the Book of Allah can be easily mastered.

It should not be considered that the meaning set forth here is exhaustive. For a deeper understanding of the meaning of the Quran, it is necessary to turn to the Sunnah of the Messenger of Allah (peace and blessings of Allah be upon him) and the classical interpretations in Arabic.

The translations and interpretations which form the basis of this book:

1. Saheeh International

2. Abridged Explanation of the Quran

3. Dr. Ghali

4. Abdul Haleem

5. Muhammad Taqi-ud-Din al-Hilali & Muhammad Muhsin Khan

6. Abu Adel

7. Tafseer-e-Baghwi

8. Ahsan-ul-Bayan

9. Taiseer-ul-Quran

10. Taiseer-ul-Rahman

11. Tafseer-e-Saadi

12. Tafseer Ibn-e-Kathir

13. Tafseer Muyassar

14. Muhammad Mohar Ali

Allah bless all the above scholars who have translated and interpreted the Quran. Allah have mercy on them.

I ask Allah to make this effort sincere, seeking His Pleasure, and I ask Him to grant us refuge in Him from the evils within us, and in our actions. I ask him to grant us success in doing what pleases Him; He is close and responsive (to the prayers of His faithful servants).

01: Surah Al-Fatiha

(The Opening)

1. (I begin) **In the name of Allah** (the most specific of the beautiful names of Allah, and no one else is called by this name), **the Most Merciful** (*Ar-Rahman* - His general mercy extends to all of His creation), **the Bestower of Mercy** (*Ar-Raheem* - Every blessing is due to His mercy, and the believers receive the greatest mercy).

2. (All) **praise is to** (only) **Allah, the Lord** (Creator, Sustainer, Ruler) **of the worlds** [of all creations],

3. **The Most Merciful, the Bestower of Mercy** (affirming the attribute of mercy to Allah as befits His Majesty. This proves the greatness and vastness of Allah's Mercy since His Mercy surrounds everything, and embraces all living beings),

4. **The** (Only) **King** [Master] **of the Day of Judgment** (the Day of Recompense for a person's actions in this world. This verse reminds a person of the Last Day, and urges him to prepare for it with

righteous deeds, and to refrain from sins and evil deeds)!

5. (Only) **You we worship and** (only) **turn to You for help** (in each and everything that only You can do). (In this verse there is evidence that the servant is not allowed to do any of the types of worship such as supplication, slaughter, and circumambulation except for Allah alone.) (All goodness is in Allah's Hand, and there is no helper except Him.)

6. **Guide us to the Straight Way** (and keep us firm on it). (This Way is Islam, which is the clear path that leads to the pleasure of Allah and to His Heaven),

صِرَاطَ ٱلَّذِينَ أَنْعَمْتَ عَلَيْهِمْ غَيْرِ ٱلْمَغْضُوبِ عَلَيْهِمْ وَلَا ٱلضَّآلِّينَ ۝

7. **The way of those whom You bestowed Your Grace** (favor, that is the way of the prophets, the truthful ones, the martyrs and the righteous. These are the people of guidance and righteousness), **not** (the way) **of those who are under** (Your) **wrath** (those who knew the truth and did not act upon it - as was the case with the Israelites), **and not** (of) **those who have gone astray** (those who have lost the true knowledge, so they wander in error, and are not guided to the Truth because they were neglectful in seeking the Truth and being guided by it – as was the case with the Christians.).

02: Surah Al-Baqarah

(The Cow)

In the name of Allah, the Most Merciful, the Bestower of Mercy.

1. **Alif Laam Meem** (These and other Arabic letters are present at the beginning of a few *surahs* – chapters - of the Quran. Only Allah knows their meaning).

ذَٰلِكَ ٱلْكِتَـٰبُ لَا رَيْبَ فِيهِ هُدًى لِّلْمُتَّقِينَ ﴿٢﴾

2. **This book** [the Quran] - **there is no doubt in it** (neither in terms of its origin, nor in terms of its meaning), [certainly it] **is a guide for those who beware** (the punishment of Allah and are mindful of Him. These are the Al-Muttaqun - the pious believers of Islamic Monotheism - who fear Allah much by abstaining from all kinds of sins and evil deeds which He has forbidden, and they love Allah much by performing all kinds of good deeds which He has ordained.),

ٱلَّذِينَ يُؤْمِنُونَ بِٱلْغَيْبِ وَيُقِيمُونَ ٱلصَّلَوٰةَ وَمِمَّا رَزَقْنَـٰهُمْ يُنفِقُونَ ﴿٣﴾

3. **who believe in the unseen** [the *Ghaib* – the unrealizable, that is the things that are beyond our senses of touch, sight, hearing etc. This includes belief in Allah, Angels, Revealed Scripture, Allah's messengers, Day of Recompense, and *Al-Qadar* - divine preordination. It also includes what Allah and His Messenger informed about the past, present and future, for example the creation of the heavens and earth, stories about the nations of the past and about Paradise and Hell etc.] **and who perform** (obligatory) **prayer, and from what We have provided them with** [from their lawful property] **they spend** (in the way of Allah as obligatory and voluntary charity) (Allah often mentions prayer and giving Zakat together. This is because prayer shows sincerity to Allah, and giving Zakat shows kindness to creation. Both are the route to happiness and success),

وَٱلَّذِينَ يُؤْمِنُونَ بِمَآ أُنزِلَ إِلَيْكَ وَمَآ أُنزِلَ مِن قَبْلِكَ وَبِٱلْآخِرَةِ هُمْ يُوقِنُونَ ﴿٤﴾

4. **who believe in what was sent down to you** (O Muhammad – peace and blessings of Allah be upon him) [in the Quran and the Sunnah - the way of the Prophet Muhammad and includes everything he said, did, and approved of] **and** (believe in) **what was sent down before you** [in the books that were sent down to the previous Prophets], **and in the Hereafter** [in the coming of the Day of Judgment, of the existence of Heaven and Hell] **they are convinced.**

أُوْلَـٰٓئِكَ عَلَىٰ هُدَى مِّن رَّبِّهِمْ ۖ وَأُوْلَـٰٓئِكَ هُمُ ٱلْمُفْلِحُونَ ۝

5. **They are on true guidance from their Lord, and they are those who have found success** (in this world and in the Eternal life – the Hereafter) (Faith in Allah and doing good actions leads to guidance and success in this world and the next).

إِنَّ ٱلَّذِينَ كَفَرُواْ سَوَآءٌ عَلَيۡهِمۡ ءَأَنذَرۡتَهُمۡ أَمۡ لَمۡ تُنذِرۡهُمۡ لَا يُؤۡمِنُونَ ۝

6. **Verily, those who** (due to their arrogance and disobedience) **disbelieve** (in what was sent down to you, O Prophet), **- it does not matter to them, whether you exhorted** [warned about the punishment of Allah] **them or did not exhort them - they will not believe.**

خَتَمَ ٱللَّهُ عَلَىٰ قُلُوبِهِمۡ وَعَلَىٰ سَمۡعِهِمۡ وَعَلَىٰٓ أَبۡصَٰرِهِمۡ غِشَٰوَةٌ وَلَهُمۡ عَذَابٌ عَظِيمٌ ۝

7. (Because they turned away from the Truth when it became clear to them) **Allah sealed their hearts and their hearing, and on their eyes, there is a**

covering [veil]. **And for them - a great punishment** (in Hell)!

وَمِنَ ٱلنَّاسِ مَن يَقُولُ ءَامَنَّا بِٱللَّهِ وَبِٱلْيَوْمِ ٱلْءَاخِرِ وَمَا هُم بِمُؤْمِنِينَ ﴿٨﴾

8. **And from** (among) **people** (there are those) **who say: "We believed in Allah and in the Last Day** [Day of Judgment].**" But they are not believers.** [These are hypocrites who are outwardly believers, but unbelievers in their souls].

يُخَٰدِعُونَ ٱللَّهَ وَٱلَّذِينَ ءَامَنُوا۟ وَمَا يَخْدَعُونَ إِلَّآ أَنفُسَهُمْ وَمَا يَشْعُرُونَ ﴿٩﴾

9. **They** [the hypocrites] **try to deceive Allah and those who believe, but they deceive only themselves, and** (themselves) **do not feel it.**

فِى قُلُوبِهِم مَّرَضٌ فَزَادَهُمُ ٱللَّهُ مَرَضًا وَلَهُمْ عَذَابٌ أَلِيمٌ بِمَا كَانُوا۟ يَكْذِبُونَ ﴿١٠﴾

10. **In their hearts** [souls] **is a disease** [of doubt], **and Allah has increased their disease! And for them - a painful punishment for the fact that they lie**.

وَإِذَا قِيلَ لَهُمْ لَا تُفْسِدُوا۟ فِى ٱلْأَرْضِ قَالُوٓا۟ إِنَّمَا نَحْنُ مُصْلِحُونَ ﴿١١﴾

11. **And when they are told: "Do not sow disorder** [unbelief, divulging the secrets of the believers, and allegiance to the unbelievers] **on the earth!" - they say: "We are only peace-makers** (people of reform)."

أَلَآ إِنَّهُمْ هُمُ ٱلْمُفْسِدُونَ وَلَـٰكِن لَّا يَشْعُرُونَ ﴿١٢﴾

12. **Oh yes! Indeed, they** [the hypocrites] **are sowing confusion, but** (they) **do not feel** (it) (they do not perceive it because of their ignorance and stubbornness).

وَإِذَا قِيلَ لَهُمْ ءَامِنُوا۟ كَمَآ ءَامَنَ ٱلنَّاسُ قَالُوٓا۟ أَنُؤْمِنُ كَمَآ ءَامَنَ ٱلسُّفَهَآءُ أَلَآ إِنَّهُمْ هُمُ ٱلسُّفَهَآءُ وَلَـٰكِن لَّا يَعْلَمُونَ ﴿١٣﴾

13. **And when they say to them** [the hypocrites]: **"Believe, as people believed** [as the companions of the Messenger of Allah – peace and blessings of Allah be upon him]!" - **they** (arguing) **answer: "Shall we believe, as the fools believed?" Oh yes** [know

that]! **Verily, they** [the hypocrites] **are** (themselves) **fools, but they** (even) **do not know** (in what error they are, that is that they do not know that they are in misguidance and loss)!

وَإِذَا لَقُواْ ٱلَّذِينَ ءَامَنُواْ قَالُوٓاْ ءَامَنَّا وَإِذَا خَلَوْاْ إِلَىٰ شَيَٰطِينِهِمْ قَالُوٓاْ إِنَّا مَعَكُمْ إِنَّمَا نَحْنُ مُسْتَهْزِءُونَ ﴿١٤﴾

14. **And when they** [the hypocrites] **meet those who have believed, they say, "We have believed!" And when they remain with their shaitans** [with their rebellious leaders, polytheist friends and soothsayers], (then) **they say: "Truly, we are with you** (united against the believers); **verily, we were but mocking** (that is belittling the believers by saying that we also believe).**"**

اللَّهُ يَسْتَهْزِئُ بِهِمْ وَيَمُدُّهُمْ فِي طُغْيَٰنِهِمْ يَعْمَهُونَ ﴿١٥﴾

15. **Allah** (Himself) **will mock them** (inflicting humiliation on them) **and He leaves them alone to increase in their wrongdoings** [delusion and doubt], **blindly wandering on.**

أُوْلَـٰئِكَ ٱلَّذِينَ ٱشْتَرَوُاْ ٱلضَّلَٰلَةَ بِٱلْهُدَىٰ فَمَا رَبِحَت تِّجَٰرَتُهُمْ وَمَا كَانُواْ مُهْتَدِينَ ﴿١٦﴾

16. **Such** [hypocrites] **are those who purchased error** [unbelief] **for** (true) **guidance** [for Faith]. **But their trade did not turn out to be profitable** (since they did not acquire anything), **and they were not guided.**

مَثَلُهُمْ كَمَثَلِ ٱلَّذِى ٱسْتَوْقَدَ نَارًا فَلَمَّآ أَضَآءَتْ مَا حَوْلَهُۥ ذَهَبَ ٱللَّهُ بِنُورِهِمْ وَتَرَكَهُمْ فِى ظُلُمَٰتٍ لَّا يُبْصِرُونَ ﴿١٧﴾

17. By example, they [the hypocrites] **are like one who** (at night) **kindled a fire** (to see the way), **and** (then) **when it illuminated everything around him, Allah took away their light** [the fire went out] **and left them in darkness so they could not see** (where to go).

صُمٌّ بُكْمٌ عُمْىٌ فَهُمْ لَا يَرْجِعُونَ ﴿١٨﴾

18. (These hypocrites**) are deaf** (to hear the truth), **dumb** (to speak it), **blind** (to see the light of the true path), **and they cannot return** (to the Faith – the Right Way).

أَوۡ كَصَيِّبٖ مِّنَ ٱلسَّمَآءِ فِيهِ ظُلُمَٰتٞ وَرَعۡدٞ وَبَرۡقٞ يَجۡعَلُونَ أَصَٰبِعَهُمۡ فِيٓ ءَاذَانِهِم مِّنَ ٱلصَّوَٰعِقِ حَذَرَ ٱلۡمَوۡتِۚ وَٱللَّهُ مُحِيطُۢ بِٱلۡكَٰفِرِينَ ﴿١٩﴾

19. **Or** (example of another group of the hypocrites) **as** (the people over whom it turned out to be) **a rain cloud from the sky.** (Then it began to rain, and) **in it is darkness, thunder and lightning, they put their fingers in their ears** (fearing) **from lightning strikes, fearing death, and Allah ever encompasses the disbelievers** (has absolute power over them, so they cannot escape Him).

يَكَادُ ٱلْبَرْقُ يَخْطَفُ أَبْصَٰرَهُمْ كُلَّمَآ أَضَآءَ لَهُم مَّشَوْا۟ فِيهِ وَإِذَآ أَظْلَمَ عَلَيْهِمْ قَامُوا۟ وَلَوْ شَآءَ ٱللَّهُ لَذَهَبَ بِسَمْعِهِمْ وَأَبْصَٰرِهِمْ إِنَّ ٱللَّهَ عَلَىٰ كُلِّ شَىْءٍ قَدِيرٌ ﴿٢٠﴾

20. **The lightning is ready to take away their sight** [they almost go blind from its brilliance]; **every time it** [lightning] **shines for them, they go with it** [by the light of lightning]. **And when darkness is over them, they stand** (in their places). **And if Allah had willed, he would have taken** [deprived] **their hearing and sight: verily, Allah is powerful over all things** [He can do everything]! (The rain could be likened to the Quran, the thunderclap to the warnings of the Quran, and the lightning to truths, which appear to the hypocrites from time to time. They covering their ears to the

thunderclaps is similar to their turning away from the truth.)

يَـٰٓأَيُّهَا ٱلنَّاسُ ٱعۡبُدُواْ رَبَّكُمُ ٱلَّذِى خَلَقَكُمۡ وَٱلَّذِينَ مِن قَبۡلِكُمۡ لَعَلَّكُمۡ تَتَّقُونَ ﴿٢١﴾

21. **O** (all) **people! Worship your Lord, who created you and those who** (were) **before you, so that** (by this) **you beware** (of the punishment of Allah)!

ٱلَّذِى جَعَلَ لَكُمُ ٱلْأَرْضَ فِرَٰشًا وَٱلسَّمَآءَ بِنَآءً وَأَنزَلَ مِنَ ٱلسَّمَآءِ مَآءً فَأَخْرَجَ بِهِۦ مِنَ ٱلثَّمَرَٰتِ رِزْقًا لَّكُمْ فَلَا تَجْعَلُوا۟ لِلَّهِ أَندَادًا وَأَنتُمْ تَعْلَمُونَ ﴿٢٢﴾

22. (Worship Him) **Who made the earth a bed for you** (so that life would be easier for you and you can rest), **and the sky as a canopy, and sent down water from the sky** (rain), **and brought out with it** [water] (different) **fruits as food for you. Do not set rivals to Allah, while you know** (that only He is the Creator and only He is worthy of worship)!

وَإِن كُنتُمْ فِي رَيْبٍ مِّمَّا نَزَّلْنَا عَلَىٰ عَبْدِنَا فَأْتُوا بِسُورَةٍ مِّن مِّثْلِهِ وَادْعُوا شُهَدَآءَكُم مِّن دُونِ اللَّهِ إِن كُنتُمْ صَٰدِقِينَ ﴿٢٣﴾

23. **And if you are in doubt about what We sent down to Our servant** [if you doubt that the Quran is from Allah], **then bring** (some) **Surah** (chapter) **of the like thereof** (and the chapter you brought should be similar to any Surah from the Quran in its beauty, meaning and benefit for Eternal Life) **and call** (for help) **your witnesses** [assistants, namely those whom you consider gods], **besides Allah, if you are truthful.**

فَإِن لَّمْ تَفْعَلُواْ وَلَن تَفْعَلُواْ فَٱتَّقُواْ ٱلنَّارَ ٱلَّتِى وَقُودُهَا ٱلنَّاسُ وَٱلْحِجَارَةُ أُعِدَّتْ لِلْكَـٰفِرِينَ ﴿٢٤﴾

24. If you do not do this - and you will never do this! - then beware of the Fire (Hell), the fuel of which (will be) **people and stones,** (which) **is prepared for the unbelievers.**

وَبَشِّرِ ٱلَّذِينَ ءَامَنُواْ وَعَمِلُواْ ٱلصَّـٰلِحَـٰتِ أَنَّ لَهُمْ جَنَّـٰتٍ تَجْرِى مِن تَحْتِهَا ٱلْأَنْهَـٰرُ كُلَّمَا رُزِقُواْ مِنْهَا مِن ثَمَرَةٍ رِّزْقًا قَالُواْ هَـٰذَا ٱلَّذِى رُزِقْنَا مِن قَبْلُ وَأُتُواْ بِهِۦ مُتَشَـٰبِهًا

وَلَهُمْ فِيهَآ أَزْوَاجٌ مُّطَهَّرَةٌ وَهُمْ فِيهَا
خَـٰلِدُونَ ﴿٢٥﴾

25. **And rejoice those who believed and did righteous deeds** [what Allah Himself and through His Messenger commanded], **that** (in Eternal Life) **for them** (there will be) **Gardens** (of Paradise), (where) **flow under which** [under the palaces and trees] **rivers. Whenever they are provided from them** [Gardens] **with (any) fruit, they say: "This is what** (already) **we were fed before"**, - **but** (when they taste it, they understand that) **is given by this** [fruit] (only) **similar to it** [resembling the old fruit] (and this one tastes even better). **And for them in them** [in the gardens of Paradise] **are pure wives** [from whom nothing unclean comes out, neither lies, nor sins, nor disobedience], **and they will abide in them** [in the Gardens of Eden] **forever** [they will not die and will not come out of there].

۞ إِنَّ ٱللَّهَ لَا يَسْتَحْيِۦٓ أَن يَضْرِبَ مَثَلًا مَّا بَعُوضَةً فَمَا فَوْقَهَا ۚ فَأَمَّا ٱلَّذِينَ ءَامَنُوا۟ فَيَعْلَمُونَ أَنَّهُ ٱلْحَقُّ مِن رَّبِّهِمْ ۖ وَأَمَّا ٱلَّذِينَ كَفَرُوا۟ فَيَقُولُونَ مَاذَآ أَرَادَ ٱللَّهُ بِهَٰذَا مَثَلًا ۘ يُضِلُّ بِهِۦ كَثِيرًا وَيَهْدِى بِهِۦ كَثِيرًا ۚ وَمَا يُضِلُّ بِهِۦٓ إِلَّا ٱلْفَٰسِقِينَ ﴿٢٦﴾

26. **Indeed, Allah does not hesitate to give an example** [as an example or parable] (even) **of a mosquito and what is higher than it** [mosquito] (to show the failure of everything that is worshiped except Allah). **As for those who believe, they know that this** [example] **is the truth from their Lord. And as for those who became unbelievers, they say: "What did Allah intend by this example?"** (Let them know that by this Allah

tests them and) **misleads many** [those who mock the truth] **and leads many by this** [increases their faith and guides them to the straight path]. **But** (Allah does not show injustice by misleading anyone) (since) **He misleads by this only the disobedient** [who disobey Him],

ٱلَّذِينَ يَنقُضُونَ عَهْدَ ٱللَّهِ مِنۢ بَعْدِ مِيثَٰقِهِۦ وَيَقْطَعُونَ مَآ أَمَرَ ٱللَّهُ بِهِۦٓ أَن يُوصَلَ وَيُفْسِدُونَ فِى ٱلْأَرْضِ أُو۟لَٰٓئِكَ هُمُ ٱلْخَٰسِرُونَ ﴿٢٧﴾

27. **Those who break the covenant of Allah** (which He took from them, that they should worship only Him and obey only Him) **after its consolidation and divide what Allah ordered to be connected, and sow confusion on the earth. Such are they who have suffered a loss** (in this world and in Eternal life).

كَيْفَ تَكْفُرُونَ بِاللَّهِ وَكُنتُمْ أَمْوَاتًا فَأَحْيَاكُمْ ثُمَّ يُمِيتُكُمْ ثُمَّ يُحْيِيكُمْ ثُمَّ إِلَيْهِ تُرْجَعُونَ ﴿٢٨﴾

28. **How do you** (O polytheists) **show disbelief in Allah** (while once) **you were dead** (before this life), **and He gave you life** [brought into this world], **then He will give you death** (and your body will be in the grave, and the angels will carry away the soul), **then He will revive you** (on the Day of Resurrection), **then you will be returned to Him** (for Judgment)?

هُوَ ٱلَّذِى خَلَقَ لَكُم مَّا فِى ٱلْأَرْضِ جَمِيعًا ثُمَّ ٱسْتَوَىٰٓ إِلَى ٱلسَّمَآءِ فَسَوَّىٰهُنَّ سَبْعَ سَمَٰوَٰتٍ وَهُوَ بِكُلِّ شَىْءٍ عَلِيمٌ ﴿٢٩﴾

29. **He** [Allah] **is the One Who created for you everything that is on earth** [all the blessings that you enjoy], **then He paid attention** (*Istawa Ila*) **towards the heaven** (sky) (in a manner which suits His Majesty), **and He arranged** [perfectly made] **them** [heavens] (in form of) **seven heavens. And He knows about everything** [He is the All-Knower]!

وَإِذْ قَالَ رَبُّكَ لِلْمَلَـٰٓئِكَةِ إِنِّى جَاعِلٌ فِى ٱلْأَرْضِ خَلِيفَةً ۖ قَالُوٓا۟ أَتَجْعَلُ فِيهَا مَن يُفْسِدُ فِيهَا وَيَسْفِكُ ٱلدِّمَآءَ وَنَحْنُ نُسَبِّحُ بِحَمْدِكَ وَنُقَدِّسُ لَكَ ۖ قَالَ إِنِّىٓ أَعْلَمُ مَا لَا تَعْلَمُونَ ﴿٣٠﴾

30. **And** (remember) **when your Lord said to the angels: "Indeed, I am going to place** (mankind) **generations after generations on the earth."** (The angels) **said:** "(O our Lord, what is the wisdom that) **You will establish on it those who** [some of them] **will therein** (also) **sow confusion and shed blood** (showing injustice and tyranny); **while we** (are obedient to You and) **glorify** (You), **giving praise to You, and we sanctify You? He said: "Indeed, I know that** [wisdom why I create people] **that you do not know!"**

وَعَلَّمَ ءَادَمَ ٱلْأَسْمَآءَ كُلَّهَا ثُمَّ عَرَضَهُمْ عَلَى ٱلْمَلَـٰٓئِكَةِ فَقَالَ أَنۢبِـُٔونِى بِأَسْمَآءِ هَـٰٓؤُلَآءِ إِن كُنتُمْ صَـٰدِقِينَ ﴿٣١﴾

31. **And** (to show the superiority of Adam over the angels) **He** [Allah] **taught Adam all the names** [names of things], **and then showed them** [the things] **to the angels and said: "Tell me the names of these** (things), **if you are truthful."**

قَالُوا۟ سُبْحَـٰنَكَ لَا عِلْمَ لَنَآ إِلَّا مَا عَلَّمْتَنَآ إِنَّكَ أَنتَ ٱلْعَلِيمُ ٱلْحَكِيمُ ﴿٣٢﴾

32. **They said** (the angels): **"Glorified are You! We have no knowledge except what You have taught us. Verily, You are the All-Knower, the**

All-Wise!" (Even if we don't know Allah's wisdom behind some of His creation or His sacred law, we must still have certain faith that there is a divine wisdom which we do not know.)

قَالَ يَـٰٓـَٔادَمُ أَنۢبِئۡهُم بِأَسۡمَآئِهِمۡ فَلَمَّآ أَنۢبَأَهُم بِأَسۡمَآئِهِمۡ قَالَ أَلَمۡ أَقُل لَّكُمۡ إِنِّىٓ أَعۡلَمُ غَيۡبَ ٱلسَّمَـٰوَٰتِ وَٱلۡأَرۡضِ وَأَعۡلَمُ مَا تُبۡدُونَ وَمَا كُنتُمۡ تَكۡتُمُونَ ﴿٣٣﴾

33. **Said** (Allah): **"O Adam, tell them** [the angels] **of their names** (which the angels did not know)!" **And** (then) **when he told them their names** (and when the superiority of Adam was manifested) **He** (Allah) **said: "Did I not tell you** [angels] **that I know the unseen** (in) **heaven and** (on) **earth and I know that what you reveal** [explicit words and deeds], **and what you hide** [your thoughts]?"

وَإِذْ قُلْنَا لِلْمَلَـٰٓئِكَةِ ٱسْجُدُوا۟ لِأَدَمَ فَسَجَدُوٓا۟ إِلَّآ إِبْلِيسَ أَبَىٰ وَٱسْتَكْبَرَ وَكَانَ مِنَ ٱلْكَـٰفِرِينَ ﴿٣٤﴾

34. **And** (remember) **when We** (Allah) **said to the angels: "Prostrate before Adam** (to show respect for him and to show his superiority)!" **And they** [the angels] **prostrated themselves, except for Iblis** (Satan), (who was a Jinn but was in the assembly of the angels, and who because of envy) **refused** (to prostrate), **and showed arrogance, and turned out to be from the disbelievers** (due to the disobedience of Allah). (Pride is the root of disobedience, and the foundation of every difficulty which was sent down upon creation.)

وَقُلْنَا يَـٰٓـَٔادَمُ ٱسْكُنْ أَنتَ وَزَوْجُكَ ٱلْجَنَّةَ وَكُلَا مِنْهَا رَغَدًا حَيْثُ شِئْتُمَا وَلَا تَقْرَبَا هَـٰذِهِ ٱلشَّجَرَةَ فَتَكُونَا مِنَ ٱلظَّـٰلِمِينَ ۩٣٥

35. **And We said: "O Adam! Settle you and your wife** (Hawwa) **in Paradise and eat** (fruits of paradise) **from there for pleasure, wherever you wish, but** (only) **do not approach this tree, so as not to be from** (among) **the wrongdoers** [who disobeyed Allah]."

فَأَزَلَّهُمَا ٱلشَّيْطَانُ عَنْهَا فَأَخْرَجَهُمَا مِمَّا كَانَا فِيهِ ۖ وَقُلْنَا ٱهْبِطُوا۟ بَعْضُكُمْ لِبَعْضٍ عَدُوٌّ ۖ وَلَكُمْ فِى ٱلْأَرْضِ مُسْتَقَرٌّ وَمَتَاعٌ إِلَىٰ حِينٍ ۝٣٦

36. **And Satan made them fall from it and brought out** [caused the expulsion] **of the two of them from where they were** [from Paradise] (Satan did not stop whispering to them. He tricked them, until he made them slip by eating from the tree which Allah had told them not to.). **And We said** (to Adam, Hawwa and Iblis): **"Go down** (to the earth), **each other** (being) **enemies! And for you on earth, a place of residence and enjoyment** (of goods) **until a** (certain) **time** [until the Day of Judgment]."

فَتَلَقَّىٰٓ ءَادَمُ مِن رَّبِّهِۦ كَلِمَـٰتٍ فَتَابَ عَلَيْهِ ۚ إِنَّهُۥ هُوَ ٱلتَّوَّابُ ٱلرَّحِيمُ ﴿٣٧﴾

37. **And Adam received from His Lord words** (so that they turn to Allah with repentance and ask His forgiveness. These words are: "Our Lord, we have wronged ourselves. If You do not forgive us and have mercy on us, we will certainly be of the losers'"), **and He** [Allah] **accepted his** [Adam's] **repentance: verily, He is the One who forgives, the Most Merciful!**

قُلْنَا ٱهْبِطُوا۟ مِنْهَا جَمِيعًا ۖ فَإِمَّا يَأْتِيَنَّكُم مِّنِّى هُدًى فَمَن تَبِعَ هُدَاىَ فَلَا خَوْفٌ عَلَيْهِمْ وَلَا هُمْ يَحْزَنُونَ ﴿٣٨﴾

38. **We** [Allah] **said: "Get down** (to earth) **from there** [from Paradise] **together! And as for the fact that** (when) **the guidance** (in which the path to the Truth is indicated) **will certainly come to you** (and to your offspring) **from Me, then there will be no fear over those who follow My guidance, and they will not grieve".**

وَٱلَّذِينَ كَفَرُواْ وَكَذَّبُواْ بِـَٔايَٰتِنَآ أُوْلَٰٓئِكَ أَصْحَٰبُ ٱلنَّارِ هُمْ فِيهَا خَٰلِدُونَ ۝

39. **And those who became unbelievers and considered Our signs a lie, those are the inhabitants of the Fire, (and) they (will) dwell in it forever.**

يَـٰبَنِىٓ إِسْرَٰٓءِيلَ ٱذْكُرُواْ نِعْمَتِىَ ٱلَّتِىٓ أَنْعَمْتُ عَلَيْكُمْ وَأَوْفُواْ بِعَهْدِىٓ أُوفِ بِعَهْدِكُمْ وَإِيَّـٰىَ فَٱرْهَبُونِ ۝

40. **O descendants of Israel! Remember My favor which I have bestowed on you, and faithfully keep My covenant, then I will also keep My covenant with you. And** (only) **fear Me.**

وَءَامِنُواْ بِمَآ أَنزَلْتُ مُصَدِّقًا لِّمَا مَعَكُمْ وَلَا تَكُونُوٓاْ أَوَّلَ كَافِرٍۭ بِهِۦ ۖ وَلَا تَشْتَرُواْ بِـَٔايَـٰتِى ثَمَنًا قَلِيلًا وَإِيَّـٰىَ فَٱتَّقُونِ ۝

41. **And believe** (O descendants of Israel, that is Yaqoob) **in the** [Quran] **that I sent down** (to Muhammad) **in confirmation of the truth of that**

[Torah] **which is with you. And do not be the first disbelievers in this** [in the Quran]. **And do not buy with My verses an insignificant price** [do not exchange My words for transient worldly goods] **and** (only) **beware of Me** (fear Me and Me alone).

وَلَا تَلْبِسُوا۟ ٱلْحَقَّ بِٱلْبَٰطِلِ وَتَكْتُمُوا۟ ٱلْحَقَّ وَأَنتُمْ تَعْلَمُونَ ۝

42. **And do not clothe the truth** (which I have explained to you) **with falsehood** (which you invented), **nor hide the truth** [the signs of the Messenger of Allah - Muhammad, which are contained in your books], **while you know** (this from your books)!

وَأَقِيمُوا۟ ٱلصَّلَوٰةَ وَءَاتُوا۟ ٱلزَّكَوٰةَ وَٱرْكَعُوا۟ مَعَ ٱلرَّٰكِعِينَ ﴿٤٣﴾

43. (Become obedient to Allah) **and pray, and give obligatory alms** [zakat], **and bow down with those who bow down** (from the community of the last messenger of Allah).

۞ أَتَأْمُرُونَ ٱلنَّاسَ بِٱلْبِرِّ وَتَنسَوْنَ أَنفُسَكُمْ وَأَنتُمْ تَتْلُونَ ٱلْكِتَٰبَ أَفَلَا تَعْقِلُونَ ﴿٤٤﴾

44. **Do you** (O descendants of Israel) **command piety** [doing righteous deeds] **to people and forget** (to admonish) **yourselves while you read the**

Scripture [Torah] (in which the signs of the Last Prophet are given)? **Don't you understand?**

وَٱسْتَعِينُوا۟ بِٱلصَّبْرِ وَٱلصَّلَوٰةِ وَإِنَّهَا لَكَبِيرَةٌ إِلَّا عَلَى ٱلْخَـٰشِعِينَ ﴿٤٥﴾

45. **And seek help** (from Allah) (in your affairs) **through patience and prayer; and, verily, it** [prayer] **is unambiguously a great burden** (for all), **except for those who are humble,**

ٱلَّذِينَ يَظُنُّونَ أَنَّهُم مُّلَـٰقُوا۟ رَبِّهِمْ وَأَنَّهُمْ إِلَيْهِ رَاجِعُونَ ﴿٤٦﴾

46. (who fear Allah and) **who know** [are convinced] **that they will meet their Lord and that they will return to Him** (on the Day of Judgment).

يَـٰبَنِىٓ إِسْرَٰٓءِيلَ ٱذْكُرُوا۟ نِعْمَتِىَ ٱلَّتِىٓ أَنْعَمْتُ عَلَيْكُمْ وَأَنِّى فَضَّلْتُكُمْ عَلَى ٱلْعَـٰلَمِينَ ﴿٤٧﴾

47. **O descendants of Israel! Remember My favor which I have bestowed you,** (and also remember) **that I gave you preference over the worlds** [those people who lived in your time].

وَٱتَّقُوا۟ يَوْمًا لَّا تَجْزِى نَفْسٌ عَن نَّفْسٍ شَيْئًا وَلَا يُقْبَلُ مِنْهَا شَفَـٰعَةٌ وَلَا يُؤْخَذُ مِنْهَا عَدْلٌ وَلَا هُمْ يُنصَرُونَ ﴿٤٨﴾

48. **And beware of the Day** [the Day of Judgment] (protect yourself from this Day by following Allah's instructions and staying away from what He has

prohibited) **when** (one) **soul will not compensate for** (help another) **soul, and intercession** (for an unbeliever) **will not be accepted** (by Allah) **from him, and compensation will not be taken from him, and they will not be helped** (in salvation from the punishment of Allah)!

وَإِذْ نَجَّيْنَـٰكُم مِّنْ ءَالِ فِرْعَوْنَ يَسُومُونَكُمْ سُوٓءَ ٱلْعَذَابِ يُذَبِّحُونَ أَبْنَآءَكُمْ وَيَسْتَحْيُونَ نِسَآءَكُمْ ۚ وَفِى ذَٰلِكُم بَلَآءٌ مِّن رَّبِّكُمْ عَظِيمٌ ۝٤٩

49. **And** (remember) **when We saved you from the people of Pharaoh, who imposed an evil punishment on you, slaughtering** [killing] (many of) **your sons and leaving your women alive. And** (it was) **in this for you a great test from your Lord!**

وَإِذْ فَرَقْنَا بِكُمُ ٱلْبَحْرَ فَأَنجَيْنَٰكُمْ
وَأَغْرَقْنَآ ءَالَ فِرْعَوْنَ وَأَنتُمْ تَنظُرُونَ ﴿٥٠﴾

50. **And** (remember) **when We separated the sea
for you** (and made a way in it), **and saved you** (from
Pharaoh and his army and also death in the water),
and drowned the people of Pharaoh (who
pursued you), **while you were watching** (how
doom befell them).

وَإِذْ وَٰعَدْنَا مُوسَىٰٓ أَرْبَعِينَ لَيْلَةً ثُمَّ ٱتَّخَذْتُمُ
ٱلْعِجْلَ مِنۢ بَعْدِهِۦ وَأَنتُمْ ظَٰلِمُونَ ﴿٥١﴾

51. **And** (remember) **when We appointed Musa** (a
period of) **forty nights** (to send down the Torah),
and then after him [after Musa left] **you took** (for

worship) **a** (golden) **calf, and you** (by doing this) **were oppressors.**

ثُمَّ عَفَوْنَا عَنكُم مِّنْ بَعْدِ ذَٰلِكَ لَعَلَّكُمْ تَشْكُرُونَ ﴿٥٢﴾

52. **Then We forgave you after that** [and accepted your repentance after the return of Musa] – **so that you may be grateful!**

وَإِذْ ءَاتَيْنَا مُوسَى ٱلْكِتَـٰبَ وَٱلْفُرْقَانَ لَعَلَّكُمْ تَهْتَدُونَ ﴿٥٣﴾

53. **And** (remember) **when We gave Musa the Scripture** [Torah] **and the Commandments** [various signs with which Allah supported Musa], **so that you** (could) **walk** (the right) **path!**

وَإِذْ قَالَ مُوسَىٰ لِقَوْمِهِ يَـٰقَوْمِ إِنَّكُمْ ظَلَمْتُمْ أَنفُسَكُم بِٱتِّخَاذِكُمُ ٱلْعِجْلَ فَتُوبُوٓاْ إِلَىٰ بَارِئِكُمْ فَٱقْتُلُوٓاْ أَنفُسَكُمْ ذَٰلِكُمْ خَيْرٌ لَّكُمْ عِندَ بَارِئِكُمْ فَتَابَ عَلَيْكُمْ إِنَّهُۥ هُوَ ٱلتَّوَّابُ ٱلرَّحِيمُ ۝

54. **And** (remember) **when Musa said to his people: "O my people! Verily, you have committed oppression in relation to yourselves by worshipping the calf. Repent then before your Creator and** (your repentance lies in the fact that you) **kill yourselves** [let those who did not worship the calf kill those who worshiped]; **that is better for you before your Creator** (than being forever in Hell). **And He accepted your repentance, verily, He is the Accepter of repentance, the Most Merciful!**

وَإِذْ قُلْتُمْ يَٰمُوسَىٰ لَن نُّؤْمِنَ لَكَ حَتَّىٰ
نَرَى ٱللَّهَ جَهْرَةً فَأَخَذَتْكُمُ ٱلصَّٰعِقَةُ
وَأَنتُمْ تَنظُرُونَ ۝

55. **And** (remember) **when you said: "O Musa! We
will not believe you** (that Allah gives you a
revelation) **until we see Allah openly** [with our
own eyes]." **And lightning struck you** [fire from
heaven] **while you were watching** (and you
perished).

ثُمَّ بَعَثْنَٰكُم مِّنۢ بَعْدِ مَوْتِكُمْ لَعَلَّكُمْ
تَشْكُرُونَ ۝

56. Then We resurrected you [revived again] **after your death** (from a lightning strike) **so that you would be grateful** (to Allah)!

وَظَلَّلْنَا عَلَيْكُمُ ٱلْغَمَامَ وَأَنزَلْنَا عَلَيْكُمُ ٱلْمَنَّ وَٱلسَّلْوَىٰ كُلُواْ مِن طَيِّبَٰتِ مَا رَزَقْنَٰكُمْ وَمَا ظَلَمُونَا وَلَٰكِن كَانُوٓاْ أَنفُسَهُمْ يَظْلِمُونَ ﴿٥٧﴾

57. And (when you wandered on the earth) **We shaded you with a cloud** [covered you under its shade] **and We sent down for you** *manna* [something like honey] **and quails.** (And We said): **"Eat the good things that We have provided for you** (and obey Allah)!" (But they began to disobey the command of Allah, did not give thanks for the blessings and lost these blessings.) **And** (thus) **they did not oppress Us, but oppressed themselves.**

وَإِذْ قُلْنَا ٱدْخُلُواْ هَـٰذِهِ ٱلْقَرْيَةَ فَكُلُواْ مِنْهَا حَيْثُ شِئْتُمْ رَغَدًا وَٱدْخُلُواْ ٱلْبَابَ سُجَّدًا وَقُولُواْ حِطَّةٌ نَّغْفِرْ لَكُمْ خَطَـٰيَـٰكُمْ وَسَنَزِيدُ ٱلْمُحْسِنِينَ ﴿٥٨﴾

58. **And** (remember) **when We said: "Enter into this village** [the city of Jerusalem] **and eat from it** [from its benefits] **where you wish, for pleasure. And enter the gate** (of this city) (showing obedience and gratitude to Allah), (namely) **bowing down, and say: "Forgiveness!** [O Allah, forgive us!]" - (and) **We will forgive you your sins and add** [increase the reward] **to the doers of good."**

فَبَدَّلَ ٱلَّذِينَ ظَلَمُواْ قَوْلًا غَيْرَ ٱلَّذِى قِيلَ لَهُمْ فَأَنزَلْنَا عَلَى ٱلَّذِينَ ظَلَمُواْ رِجْزًا مِّنَ ٱلسَّمَآءِ بِمَا كَانُواْ يَفْسُقُونَ ﴿٥٩﴾

59. **And those who committed oppression** (the wrongdoers from among the descendants of Israel) **replaced** (the word of Allah) **with a word other than what was told to them. And We sent down upon those who committed oppression a punishment from heaven because they were disobedient.**

۞ وَإِذِ ٱسْتَسْقَىٰ مُوسَىٰ لِقَوْمِهِۦ فَقُلْنَا ٱضْرِب بِّعَصَاكَ ٱلْحَجَرَ فَٱنفَجَرَتْ مِنْهُ ٱثْنَتَا عَشْرَةَ عَيْنًا قَدْ عَلِمَ كُلُّ أُنَاسٍ مَّشْرَبَهُمْ كُلُواْ وَٱشْرَبُواْ مِن رِّزْقِ ٱللَّهِ وَلَا

تَعْثَوْاْ فِى ٱلْأَرْضِ مُفْسِدِينَ ﴿٦٠﴾

60. **And** (remember) **when Musa** (peace be upon him) **asked for water for his people** (turning to Allah with a prayer) (when you wandered in the wilderness), **and We** (Allah) **said** (to Musa): **"Strike your staff on a stone!"** (And Musa struck) **and twelve springs gushed out of it** (in accordance to the number of the tribes of the descendants of Israel), **so that every tribe** (community of people) **knew their drinking place.** [Each tribe had its own source, so that there would be no disputes between the clans]. (And We said): **"Eat and drink from the provision of Allah! And do not run amok on the earth, sowing disorder** (making mischief and corruption)."

وَإِذْ قُلْتُمْ يَٰمُوسَىٰ لَن نَّصْبِرَ عَلَىٰ طَعَامٍ
وَٰحِدٍ فَٱدْعُ لَنَا رَبَّكَ يُخْرِجْ لَنَا مِمَّا
تُنۢبِتُ ٱلْأَرْضُ مِنۢ بَقْلِهَا وَقِثَّآئِهَا وَفُومِهَا
وَعَدَسِهَا وَبَصَلِهَا قَالَ أَتَسْتَبْدِلُونَ ٱلَّذِى
هُوَ أَدْنَىٰ بِٱلَّذِى هُوَ خَيْرٌ ٱهْبِطُواْ مِصْرًا
فَإِنَّ لَكُم مَّا سَأَلْتُمْ وَضُرِبَتْ عَلَيْهِمُ
ٱلذِّلَّةُ وَٱلْمَسْكَنَةُ وَبَآءُو بِغَضَبٍ مِّنَ ٱللَّهِ
ذَٰلِكَ بِأَنَّهُمْ كَانُواْ يَكْفُرُونَ بِـَٔايَٰتِ ٱللَّهِ
وَيَقْتُلُونَ ٱلنَّبِيِّـۧنَ بِغَيْرِ ٱلْحَقِّ ذَٰلِكَ بِمَا
عَصَواْ وَّكَانُواْ يَعْتَدُونَ ۝

61. **And** (remember) **when you said** (when We sent down to you, O descendants of Israel, blessed food): **"O Musa! We cannot tolerate the same food** [eating the same]. **So turn with a prayer for us to your Lord, let Him bring out to us what the earth grows from its vegetables, cucumbers, garlic** (or wheat), **lentils and onions.** (And Musa) **said: "Are you asking to replace what is lower** [worse] [ordinary food] **with what is better** [what Allah has chosen as food for you]**? Go down** (from the desert) **to** (any) **city, and verily** (there) **for you** (there will be) [that food] **that you asked for". And humiliation and poverty were brought down over them. And they returned** [turned] **under the wrath of Allah** (became deserving of Allah's wrath). **This** [what is listed above] **is because they were showing disbelief in the signs of Allah and killing the Prophets without the right** [without having the right to do so, that is unjustly]! **This is because they disobeyed** (Allah) **and were transgressors** (limits set by Allah)!

إِنَّ ٱلَّذِينَ ءَامَنُواْ وَٱلَّذِينَ هَادُواْ وَٱلنَّصَٰرَىٰ وَٱلصَّٰبِـِٔينَ مَنْ ءَامَنَ بِٱللَّهِ وَٱلْيَوْمِ ٱلْأَخِرِ وَعَمِلَ صَٰلِحًا فَلَهُمْ أَجْرُهُمْ عِندَ رَبِّهِمْ وَلَا خَوْفٌ عَلَيْهِمْ وَلَا هُمْ يَحْزَنُونَ ﴿٦٢﴾

62. **Verily, those who believed** (from the community of the Last Prophet Muhammad – peace and blessings of Allah be upon him), **and those who** (before Allah sent the last Prophet, that is from the communities who came before the Last and Final Prophet) **were Jews, and Christians, and Sabians** [those who are in the natural faith from birth], **who believes** (of them) **in Allah and on the Last Day and does righteousness, then they** (will have) **their reward with their Lord, and there will be no fear over them** (on the Day of Resurrection), **and they will not grieve** (for what passed them in this life). (Now after Prophet

Muhammad was sent, his message of Islam is the only way of life accepted by Allah, as He said in the Quran: 'Whoever seeks a path other than Islam, it will not be accepted from him'. Surah Al Imran: 85).

وَإِذْ أَخَذْنَا مِيثَٰقَكُمْ وَرَفَعْنَا فَوْقَكُمُ ٱلطُّورَ خُذُواْ مَآ ءَاتَيْنَٰكُم بِقُوَّةٍ وَٱذْكُرُواْ مَا فِيهِ لَعَلَّكُمْ تَتَّقُونَ ﴿٦٣﴾

63. **And** (remember) **when We took an agreement with you** (that you will believe in Allah and worship only Him) **and raised mountain above you** (and We said to you): **"Take** [Torah] **that We have given you, with strength** [with zeal] (and keep it) **and remember what is in it** [in the Scripture], **so that** (by this) **you beware** (of the punishment of Allah)!

ثُمَّ تَوَلَّيۡتُم مِّنۢ بَعۡدِ ذَٰلِكَ فَلَوۡلَا فَضۡلُ ٱللَّهِ عَلَيۡكُمۡ وَرَحۡمَتُهُۥ لَكُنتُم مِّنَ ٱلۡخَٰسِرِينَ ﴿٦٤﴾

64. **Then you turned away after that** [after accepting the treaty and raising the mountain above you] **and, if not for the favor of Allah to you and His mercy** (that He allowed repentance), **then you would definitely be from** (number) **of those who have suffered loss** (both in this world and in Eternal life).

وَلَقَدۡ عَلِمۡتُمُ ٱلَّذِينَ ٱعۡتَدَوۡاْ مِنكُمۡ فِى ٱلسَّبۡتِ فَقُلۡنَا لَهُمۡ كُونُواْ قِرَدَةً خَٰسِـِٔينَ ﴿٦٥﴾

65. **And certainly you** (O descendants of Israel) **knew** (about) **those of you** (who lived before and) **who transgressed** (the prohibition) **on the Sabbath** (and what happened to them). **And** (after that) **We said to them: "Be despicable monkeys!"** (And turned them into monkeys). (Allah sometimes punishes disobedient people in this life itself, as a way of cautioning other people, so that they don't go against Allah's sacred law. Not obeying Allah's commands and trying to cheat the sacred law is forbidden, because Allah can never be deceived.)

فَجَعَلْنَٰهَا نَكَٰلًا لِّمَا بَيْنَ يَدَيْهَا وَمَا خَلْفَهَا وَمَوْعِظَةً لِّلْمُتَّقِينَ ﴿٦٦﴾

66. **And We made it** [that village] **a deterrent punishment for those** (villages) **that are in front of this** (village) [who are close], **and those behind it** [to whom the news of this punishment will reach], **and a lesson for those who fear Allah.**

وَإِذْ قَالَ مُوسَىٰ لِقَوْمِهِۦٓ إِنَّ ٱللَّهَ يَأْمُرُكُمْ أَن تَذْبَحُواْ بَقَرَةً قَالُوٓاْ أَتَتَّخِذُنَا هُزُوًا قَالَ أَعُوذُ بِٱللَّهِ أَنْ أَكُونَ مِنَ ٱلْجَٰهِلِينَ ﴿٦٧﴾

67. **And** (remember O Children of Israel the crime of your ancestors, and their many stubbornness and their arguments against Moses) **when Musa said** (having received a revelation from Allah) **to his people: "Indeed, Allah orders you to slaughter** (any) **cow."** (Instead of hurrying to do so and obey the command of Allah, stubbornly) **They said: "Are you mocking** (making fun of) **us?" He** [Musa] **said: "I turn** (for protection) **to Allah, so as not to be from** (among) **the ignorant!"**

قَالُوا۟ ٱدْعُ لَنَا رَبَّكَ يُبَيِّن لَّنَا مَا هِىَ قَالَ إِنَّهُۥ يَقُولُ إِنَّهَا بَقَرَةٌ لَّا فَارِضٌ وَلَا بِكْرٌ عَوَانٌ بَيْنَ ذَٰلِكَ فَٱفْعَلُوا۟ مَا تُؤْمَرُونَ ۝٦٨

68. **They said** (although the command was clear): **"Please pray for us to your Lord, so that He will explain to us what it is."** He [Prophet Musa] **said: "Indeed, He [Allah] says that it is a cow, not old and not young, middle in age between these."** (And Musa said): **"So do what you are ordered!"**

قَالُوا۟ ٱدْعُ لَنَا رَبَّكَ يُبَيِّن لَّنَا مَا لَوْنُهَا قَالَ إِنَّهُۥ يَقُولُ إِنَّهَا بَقَرَةٌ صَفْرَآءُ فَاقِعٌ لَّوْنُهَا تَسُرُّ ٱلنَّٰظِرِينَ ۝٦٩

69. (They continued debating and again showed stubbornness) **They said: "Turn with a prayer for us to your Lord** (call upon Allah), **so that He explains to us what its color is."** (Musa) **said: "Verily, He** [Allah] **says that she is a yellow cow,** (and) **her color** [without spots] **is bright** [pure], (and) **pleases** (she) **those who look** (at her)."** (When people would make easy matters of the sacred law more difficult and stricter for themselves then Allah would sometimes make things even stricter for them as a result.)

قَالُواْ ٱدۡعُ لَنَا رَبَّكَ يُبَيِّن لَّنَا مَا هِىَ إِنَّ ٱلۡبَقَرَ تَشَـٰبَهَ عَلَيۡنَا وَإِنَّآ إِن شَآءَ ٱللَّهُ لَمُهۡتَدُونَ ﴿٧٠﴾

70. **They said** (being stubborn for the third time): **"Turn with a prayer for us to your Lord, so that He explains to us what it is** [they wanted more

signs]. **Verily, cows are similar to each other for us** (they look alike to us), **and verily, if Allah wills, we will definitely be on the right path** (we will be guided when we look for the cow that should be sacrificed).

قَالَ إِنَّهُۥ يَقُولُ إِنَّهَا بَقَرَةٌ لَّا ذَلُولٌ تُثِيرُ ٱلْأَرْضَ وَلَا تَسْقِى ٱلْحَرْثَ مُسَلَّمَةٌ لَّا شِيَةَ فِيهَا قَالُوا۟ ٱلْـَٰٔنَ جِئْتَ بِٱلْحَقِّ فَذَبَحُوهَا وَمَا كَادُوا۟ يَفْعَلُونَ ﴿٧١﴾

71. **He** (Musa**) said: "Truly, He** (Allah) **says that it is a cow, not tamed, which** (does not) **plow the ground, and does not irrigate the arable land, kept intact** [without flaws], **there is no mark** [a spot of another color] **on her." They said, "Now you have delivered the truth** [full explanation]." (And they realized that he was not mocking them.)

And they slaughtered her [the cow], **although they were ready not to do it** (they did not do it with good will due to all their arguing and stubbornness. They slaughtered it after a lengthy evasion.).

وَإِذْ قَتَلْتُمْ نَفْسًا فَٱدَّٰرَأْتُمْ فِيهَا ۖ وَٱللَّهُ مُخْرِجٌ مَّا كُنتُمْ تَكْتُمُونَ ﴿٧٢﴾

72. **And** (remember that event) **when you** (O descendants of Israel) **killed the soul** [of a person] **and you argued about it** (the crime), **and Allah was to bring out** [revealed] **what you hid.**

فَقُلْنَا ٱضْرِبُوهُ بِبَعْضِهَا ۚ كَذَٰلِكَ يُحْيِ ٱللَّهُ ٱلْمَوْتَىٰ وَيُرِيكُمْ ءَايَٰتِهِۦ لَعَلَّكُمْ تَعْقِلُونَ ﴿٧٣﴾

73. **And We said** (by revelation to Musa, so that he conveyed to them): **"Strike him** [the person who was killed] **with something** [part] **from it** [from the sacrificed cow]." (And the victim, after a blow to him, came to life and said the name of the killer). **This is how Allah will revive the dead** (on the Day of Resurrection) **and show you His signs** (in this world) **so that you understand** (and be deterred from doing sins which harm you)!

ثُمَّ قَسَتْ قُلُوبُكُم مِّن بَعْدِ ذَٰلِكَ فَهِىَ كَٱلْحِجَارَةِ أَوْ أَشَدُّ قَسْوَةً وَإِنَّ مِنَ ٱلْحِجَارَةِ لَمَا يَتَفَجَّرُ مِنْهُ ٱلْأَنْهَٰرُ وَإِنَّ مِنْهَا لَمَا يَشَّقَّقُ فَيَخْرُجُ مِنْهُ ٱلْمَآءُ وَإِنَّ

مِنْهَا لَمَا يَهْبِطُ مِنْ خَشْيَةِ ٱللَّهِ وَمَا ٱللَّهُ بِغَٰفِلٍ عَمَّا تَعْمَلُونَ ﴿٧٤﴾

74. **Then** [after Allah showed you miracles and blessed you with numerous blessings your hearts should have softened and become humble but instead] **your hearts hardened after that** (your hearts did not benefit): **they** [hearts] **became like stones or** (even) **more cruel** (worse in hardness). **And, verily, among the stones, unequivocally, there are** [some] **from which rivers gush forth. And, verily, among them, unequivocally, there are those that are split, and water comes out from them** (like, for example, stones in wells). **And, verily, among them, unequivocally, there are those who fall down from fear of Allah. And Allah** (is) **not unaware about what you do!** (Allah keeps a record of all your actions and He will recompense you for them on the Day of Judgment).

أَفَتَطْمَعُونَ أَن يُؤْمِنُوا لَكُمْ وَقَدْ كَانَ فَرِيقٌ مِّنْهُمْ يَسْمَعُونَ كَلَمَ اللَّهِ ثُمَّ يُحَرِّفُونَهُۥ مِنۢ بَعْدِ مَا عَقَلُوهُ وَهُمْ يَعْلَمُونَ ۝٧٥

75. **Do you** (O believers) **hope** (very desiring) **that they** [Jews] **believe you, while there was already a party among them** [experts in their teachings – the Jewish Rabbis], **who listened to the speech** [words] **of Allah** (from the Torah), **and then they distorted it** [changed the meaning], **after they comprehended it** [realizing that it is the truth], **and they** (did it) **knowingly** (they did it deliberately being fully aware of the seriousness of the crime)? (O believers, do not expect from them that they will become Muslims, after knowing their true nature and how stubborn they are. They won't be truthful and it is

highly unlikely that they will respond to your call of Islam.)

وَإِذَا لَقُواْ ٱلَّذِينَ ءَامَنُواْ قَالُوٓاْ ءَامَنَّا وَإِذَا خَلَا بَعْضُهُمْ إِلَىٰ بَعْضٍ قَالُوٓاْ أَتُحَدِّثُونَهُم بِمَا فَتَحَ ٱللَّهُ عَلَيْكُمْ لِيُحَآجُّوكُم بِهِۦ عِندَ رَبِّكُمْ أَفَلَا تَعْقِلُونَ ﴿٧٦﴾

76. **And when they** [the Jews] **met those who believed** (in Allah, the One and only True God, the Quran, Allah's last Messenger Muhammad, and the Last Day**), they said: "We have believed!"** (Some of the Jews met some Muslims and acknowledged the truth of the Prophet Muhammad - peace be upon him - and the correctness of his message according to the Torah.) **And when some of them** [from the Jews] **were alone with others, they said: "Do you really tell them** [believers] **what Allah** (in the

Torah) **revealed to you** [the Jews] (regarding the signs of the Last Prophet Muhammad – peace and blessings of Allah be upon him - which are written in the Torah), **so that** (later) **they began to argue against you by means of this before your Lord** (on the Day of Judgment)? (The Muslims may use what these Jews told them as proof that they recognized the truth of Muhammad's prophethood.) **Don't you understand?"**

أَوَلَا يَعْلَمُونَ أَنَّ ٱللَّهَ يَعْلَمُ مَا يُسِرُّونَ وَمَا يُعْلِنُونَ ۝

77. **Don't they** [Jews] **know that Allah knows both what they hide** (in their souls) **and what they reveal** [do openly]**?** (Allah knows and exposed their true nature to His slaves)

وَمِنْهُمْ أُمِّيُّونَ لَا يَعْلَمُونَ ٱلْكِتَـٰبَ إِلَّآ أَمَانِيَّ وَإِنْ هُمْ إِلَّا يَظُنُّونَ ۝

78. **And among them** [the People of the Book – the Jews and Christians] **there are illiterates who do not know the Scriptures** [cannot read and write and therefore do not know what is written in their books such as Torah], **but** (they believe) **only wishful thinking** [stories without any basis. This also applies to those who don't read the Quran with understanding.] (These common folks only know lies which they heard from some of their leaders, and think it is the Torah revealed by Allah, and then tell these lies to others). **And they only speculate** [they only assume and guess since they have no true knowledge of the contents of the Book that Allah has revealed to them]. (So the scholars among them were following the verses of their scriptures which they themselves had changed the meaning of, and the common folks among them were blindly following the scholars

without asking for authentic evidence. Therefore, there is no hope that either of them will believe in the message of Islam.)

فَوَيْلٌ لِّلَّذِينَ يَكْتُبُونَ ٱلْكِتَـٰبَ بِأَيْدِيهِمْ ثُمَّ يَقُولُونَ هَـٰذَا مِنْ عِندِ ٱللَّهِ لِيَشْتَرُواْ بِهِۦ ثَمَنًا قَلِيلًا ۖ فَوَيْلٌ لَّهُم مِّمَّا كَتَبَتْ أَيْدِيهِمْ وَوَيْلٌ لَّهُم مِّمَّا يَكْسِبُونَ ﴿٧٩﴾

79. **Woe** (misery, death, great suffering, and destruction) **to those who write the Scripture [Torah] with their own hands** [change it] **and then say: "This is from Allah," in order to buy** [take] **by this** [distortion and rewriting] **a small price** [for worldly values such as money or leadership that are insignificant compared to the values of Eternal Life]! **Woe to them for what their hands have written** (through which they told lies about Allah),

and woe to them for what they gain (earn because of what lies their hands had written)! (By changing the scriptures, they propagate falsehood and hide the truth.) (Shaikh al-Islam Ibn Taymiyyah – Allah have mercy on him – said that Allah has condemned those who distort His Words, and this includes those who explain or teach the Quran and the Sunnah on the basis of innovation – *Bid'ah* – that is they teach something new in Islam which has not been taught by Allah or Prophet Muhammad – peace and blessings of Allah be upon him.)

وَقَالُواْ لَن تَمَسَّنَا ٱلنَّارُ إِلَّآ أَيَّامًا مَّعْدُودَةً قُلْ أَتَّخَذْتُمْ عِندَ ٱللَّهِ عَهْدًا فَلَن يُخْلِفَ ٱللَّهُ عَهْدَهُۥٓ أَمْ تَقُولُونَ عَلَى ٱللَّهِ مَا لَا تَعْلَمُونَ ﴿٨٠﴾

80. And they [the Jews] **said** (falsely): **"Fire will not touch us except for a few days."** [They think they won't stay in Hell forever. They did evil things thinking that they will be no consequences.]. **Say** (to them) (O Prophet): **"Have you taken an agreement** [made a covenant or promise] (about this) **from Allah?** (If you have indeed entered into such an agreement, then know that) **Allah will never violate His agreement. Or do you speak against Allah that which you do not know?"** (This nullifies their claim and Allah exposes them - that they are fabricators and liars and speak regarding Allah without any evidence. Speaking about Allah without knowledge is one of the greatest forbidden actions which is most abhorrent.)

بَلَىٰ مَن كَسَبَ سَيِّئَةً وَأَحَـٰطَتْ بِهِۦ خَطِيٓـَٔتُهُۥ فَأُو۟لَـٰٓئِكَ أَصْحَـٰبُ ٱلنَّارِ هُمْ فِيهَا خَـٰلِدُونَ ﴿٨١﴾

81. **Nay!** [Not the way you say]. (On the contrary) **Whoever acquired evil** [committed unbelief – polytheism or atheism] **and who was surrounded** [embraced] **by his sin** (of unbelief – associating partners with Allah – which prevents him from accepting Islam and repenting), **then those are the inhabitants of the Fire [Hell], they abide in it forever** (eternally).

وَٱلَّذِينَ ءَامَنُواْ وَعَمِلُواْ ٱلصَّٰلِحَٰتِ أُوْلَٰٓئِكَ أَصْحَٰبُ ٱلْجَنَّةِ هُمْ فِيهَا خَٰلِدُونَ ﴿٨٢﴾

82. **And those who believed** (in Allah, His Messengers, His Angels, His Books, and the Last Day) **and did righteous deeds** [performed only for the sake of Allah what Allah Himself commanded directly and through His Messenger. The deeds should be in accordance with the Sunnah of the Messenger – peace and blessings of Allah be upon him], **such are the**

**inhabitants of Paradise, they (will) stay in it
forever.**

وَإِذْ أَخَذْنَا مِيثَاقَ بَنِىٓ إِسْرَٰٓءِيلَ لَا
تَعْبُدُونَ إِلَّا ٱللَّهَ وَبِٱلْوَٰلِدَيْنِ إِحْسَانًا
وَذِى ٱلْقُرْبَىٰ وَٱلْيَتَٰمَىٰ وَٱلْمَسَٰكِينِ وَقُولُوا۟
لِلنَّاسِ حُسْنًا وَأَقِيمُوا۟ ٱلصَّلَوٰةَ وَءَاتُوا۟
ٱلزَّكَوٰةَ ثُمَّ تَوَلَّيْتُمْ إِلَّا قَلِيلًا مِّنكُمْ
وَأَنتُم مُّعْرِضُونَ ﴿٨٣﴾

83. And (remember) **when** (through the prophets)
**We took an agreement with the descendants of
Israel** (and this covenant was that): **"You will not
worship anyone but Allah** (alone. This is the right
of Allah); **and towards parents you will do good**
(be kind to them in words and actions), **and** (also)

towards the possessor of kinship [relatives], **and towards orphans, and towards the poor** (needy). **And speak good** [good words without harshness or severity] **to people** (say words of righteousness and forbid evil, and say the truth about Muhammad – peace and blessings of Allah be upon him), **and pray** (properly), **and give obligatory alms** [zakat]." **Then you turned away** (from this agreement), **except for a few of you** (not all of them turned away and Allah protected a few of them and made them steadfast), **and you** (were at the same time) **refusing.**

وَإِذْ أَخَذْنَا مِيثَاقَكُمْ لَا تَسْفِكُونَ دِمَاءَكُمْ وَلَا تُخْرِجُونَ أَنفُسَكُم مِّن دِيَارِكُمْ ثُمَّ أَقْرَرْتُمْ وَأَنتُمْ تَشْهَدُونَ ﴿٨٤﴾

84. **And** (remember) **when We took a covenant from you** (in the Torah) (O descendants of Israel),

(that) **you will not shed your blood** [one of you will not kill other of you] **and** (that) **you will not drive yourselves** [each other] **out of your dwellings** [native places]. **Then you** (referring to the Jews of Madinah) **confirmed** (acknowledged this covenant), **while you yourself testified** (that this is in your creed).

ثُمَّ أَنتُمْ هَـٰؤُلَاءِ تَقْتُلُونَ أَنفُسَكُمْ وَتُخْرِجُونَ فَرِيقًا مِّنكُم مِّن دِيَـٰرِهِمْ تَظَـٰهَرُونَ عَلَيْهِم بِٱلْإِثْمِ وَٱلْعُدْوَٰنِ وَإِن يَأْتُوكُمْ أُسَـٰرَىٰ تُفَـٰدُوهُمْ وَهُوَ مُحَرَّمٌ

عَلَيْكُمْ إِخْرَاجُهُمْ أَفَتُؤْمِنُونَ بِبَعْضِ
الْكِتَٰبِ وَتَكْفُرُونَ بِبَعْضٍ فَمَا جَزَآءُ
مَن يَفْعَلُ ذَٰلِكَ مِنكُمْ إِلَّا خِزْىٌ فِى
الْحَيَوٰةِ الدُّنْيَا وَيَوْمَ الْقِيَٰمَةِ يُرَدُّونَ إِلَىٰٓ أَشَدِّ
الْعَذَابِ وَمَا اللَّهُ بِغَٰفِلٍ عَمَّا تَعْمَلُونَ ﴿٨٥﴾

85. **Then you** (O Jews), **kill yourselves** [kill one another and break the covenant] (when two Arab tribes were at war with each other, and one of you was allies of one tribe, and the other of another tribe**) and drive one party out of you** [the Jews] **from their dwellings, helping** (their enemies) **against them** [against your brothers] **with sin and enmity** [without having the right to do so]. **And if** (after the war) **they come to you as prisoners, you ransom them** (in order to free them from captivity), **while it is forbidden for you** (first of all) **to expel them**

(from their dwellings). **Do you believe in one part of Scripture** [Torah] (that it is allowed to ransom captives) **and show disbelief in the other** (part, that is not killing fellow tribesmen and expelling them as a sin)? **There is no recompense for those who do this of you, except for disgrace in the worldly life, and on the Day of Resurrection they will be returned to the most severe punishment** [in Hell]! **And Allah is not unaware about what you do!** (Allah will hold them to account for their actions.)

أُوْلَـٰئِكَ ٱلَّذِينَ ٱشْتَرَوُاْ ٱلْحَيَوٰةَ ٱلدُّنْيَا بِٱلْأَخِرَةِ فَلَا يُخَفَّفُ عَنْهُمُ ٱلْعَذَابُ وَلَا هُمْ يُنصَرُونَ ﴿٨٦﴾

86. **Such** [Jews who violated the agreement with Allah] **are those who bought** [choose] **the life of this world** (in exchange) **for Eternal life, and**

their punishment will not be lightened, and they will not be helped [no one can avert the punishment of Allah from them].

وَلَقَدۡ ءَاتَيۡنَا مُوسَى ٱلۡكِتَـٰبَ وَقَفَّيۡنَا مِنۢ بَعۡدِهِۦ بِٱلرُّسُلِۖ وَءَاتَيۡنَا عِيسَى ٱبۡنَ مَرۡيَمَ ٱلۡبَيِّنَـٰتِ وَأَيَّدۡنَـٰهُ بِرُوحِ ٱلۡقُدُسِۗ أَفَكُلَّمَا جَآءَكُمۡ رَسُولٌۢ بِمَا لَا تَهۡوَىٰٓ أَنفُسُكُمُ ٱسۡتَكۡبَرۡتُمۡ فَفَرِيقًا كَذَّبۡتُمۡ وَفَرِيقًا تَقۡتُلُونَ ۝٨٧

87. **And** (most certainly) **indeed We gave** (the prophet) **Musa the Scripture** [Torah] **and We sent** (to the descendants of Israel**) after him** [after Musa] **messengers; and We gave Jesus the son of Maryam clear signs** (which indicate that he is the Messenger of Allah - such as bringing the dead back to

life with the permission of Allah, and healing the blind and the lepers) **and We supported him with the Holy Spirit** [the angel Jibril]. **Every time a messenger** (with a revelation from Allah**) comes to you with something** [with legal provisions] **that your souls do not desire,** (then) **you show arrogance. Some of them you considered as liars** (like Jesus and Muhammad – peace and blessings of Allah be upon him), **and others you kill** (like Zakariya and Yahya). (It is from Allah's mercy to His creation that He sent many messengers and scriptures to guide them.)

وَقَالُواْ قُلُوبُنَا غُلْفٌ ۚ بَل لَّعَنَهُمُ ٱللَّهُ بِكُفْرِهِمْ فَقَلِيلًا مَّا يُؤْمِنُونَ ﴿٨٨﴾

88. **And they** [the descendants of Israel] **said** (justifying their refusal to accept what the Messenger of Allah had come with): **"Our hearts are covered**

[covered with something] (and therefore the truth does not reach us)." **But no** [these arguments are untenable]! **Allah cursed them** [deprived them of His mercy] **for their disbelief; so little it is that they believe!** (Those who turn away from guidance and stubbornly refuse to obey the commands of Allah are punished by Allah with a seal on their hearts, thus depriving them of His mercy. Because of this they will not be guided to the truth, and will not act according to it.)

وَلَمَّا جَآءَهُمْ كِتَـٰبٌ مِّنْ عِندِ ٱللَّهِ مُصَدِّقٌ لِّمَا مَعَهُمْ وَكَانُوا۟ مِن قَبْلُ يَسْتَفْتِحُونَ عَلَى ٱلَّذِينَ كَفَرُوا۟ فَلَمَّا جَآءَهُم مَّا عَرَفُوا۟ كَفَرُوا۟ بِهِۦ ۚ فَلَعْنَةُ ٱللَّهِ عَلَى ٱلْكَـٰفِرِينَ ﴿٨٩﴾

89. **And when it came to them** [to the Jews] (another) **scripture from Allah** [Quran], **confirming the truth of what is with them** [Torah], **- and even before** [before Allah sent the last prophet] **they asked** (prayed to Allah and sought His help against the polytheists of the Arabs, saying: The coming of the Last Prophet is near at the end of time, and we will follow him and fight against you) **for victory against those who became unbelievers** [against the pagan polytheists] **- and when it came to them** [to the Jews] **what they knew** (from their books) [when the last messenger came and the Quran began to be sent down], **they showed disbelief in it** (rejected the last Prophet out of envy and resentment). **The curse of Allah is on the disbelievers!**

بِئْسَمَا ٱشْتَرَوْاْ بِهِۦٓ أَنفُسَهُمْ أَن يَكْفُرُواْ بِمَآ أَنزَلَ ٱللَّهُ بَغْيًا أَن يُنَزِّلَ ٱللَّهُ مِن فَضْلِهِۦ عَلَىٰ مَن يَشَآءُ مِنْ عِبَادِهِۦ فَبَآءُو بِغَضَبٍ عَلَىٰ غَضَبٍ وَلِلْكَٰفِرِينَ عَذَابٌ مُّهِينٌ ﴿٩٠﴾

90. **It is evil** [disbelief] **for which they** [the descendants of Israel] **sold** (their souls) **themselves, that they showed disbelief in what Allah sent down** [in the Quran], **out of envy that Allah sends down from His generosity to whomever He wants from His servants** [out of envy of the Prophet Muhammad – peace and blessings of Allah be upon him]! **And they returned** (having drawn upon themselves the deserving) **anger** (of Allah) **against** (already existing) **anger** (which was on them for their former manifestations of disbelief). **And** (prepared) **for the disbelievers is a humiliating punishment!**

وَإِذَا قِيلَ لَهُمْ ءَامِنُواْ بِمَآ أَنزَلَ ٱللَّهُ قَالُواْ نُؤْمِنُ بِمَآ أُنزِلَ عَلَيْنَا وَيَكْفُرُونَ بِمَا وَرَآءَهُۥ وَهُوَ ٱلْحَقُّ مُصَدِّقًا لِّمَا مَعَهُمْ قُلْ فَلِمَ تَقْتُلُونَ أَنۢبِيَآءَ ٱللَّهِ مِن قَبْلُ إِن كُنتُم مُّؤْمِنِينَ ۞ ٩١

91. **And when it is said to them** [the Jews]: **"Believe in what Allah sent down** [in the Quran]!**"** - **they say: "We believe in what has been sent down to us** [in the Torah].**" And they deny in that which comes after it** [in the Quran], **although this** [Quran] **is the truth, confirming the truth of that** [Torah] **that is with them** [with the Jews]. **Say** (to them O Messenger): **"Why did you kill the prophets of Allah before, if you are believers** [if you believe in what Allah revealed to you]?**"**

﷽ وَلَقَدْ جَآءَكُم مُّوسَىٰ بِٱلْبَيِّنَٰتِ ثُمَّ ٱتَّخَذْتُمُ ٱلْعِجْلَ مِنۢ بَعْدِهِۦ وَأَنتُمْ ظَٰلِمُونَ ﴿٩٢﴾

92. **And** (certainly) **indeed** (O Jews) (the Prophet) **Musa came to you with clear signs** [evidence that he is the true Messenger of Allah —clear miracles indicative of his truthfulness, such as the flood, locusts, lice, frogs, and other things that Allah mentioned in the Quran], **then you took** (for yourself) **a** (golden) **calf** (to worship) **after him** [after Musa went to the place appointed by Allah], **and you** (were) **oppressors** (polytheists and wrongdoer because you dedicated worship to someone or something who did not deserve it and went beyond the limits set by Allah. The Jews had promised that they would worship Allah alone and not do *shirk* – that is associate partners with Allah.).

وَإِذْ أَخَذْنَا مِيثَٰقَكُمْ وَرَفَعْنَا فَوْقَكُمُ
ٱلطُّورَ خُذُوا۟ مَآ ءَاتَيْنَٰكُم بِقُوَّةٍ وَٱسْمَعُوا۟
قَالُوا۟ سَمِعْنَا وَعَصَيْنَا وَأُشْرِبُوا۟ فِى قُلُوبِهِمُ
ٱلْعِجْلَ بِكُفْرِهِمْ قُلْ بِئْسَمَا يَأْمُرُكُم
بِهِۦٓ إِيمَٰنُكُمْ إِن كُنتُم مُّؤْمِنِينَ ﴿٩٣﴾

93. **And** (remember) **when We took an agreement**
(covenant) **with you** (O descendants of Israel) (that
you will believe in Allah and worship only Him) **and
raised the mountain** (Tur) **above you** (and We
said): **"Take that** [Torah] **which We have given
you with strength** [with zeal and determination]
(and keep it) **and listen** (what is commanded in it and
obey the commandments)! **They said: "We heard**
(this with our ears) **and disobeyed** (this with our
actions)." **And they were drunk in their hearts
with the calf** [their hearts absorbed the love of the

calf] **because of their unbelief. Say: "It is wretched** [the worship of the calf] **that which your faith commands you, if you** (at all) **are believers!"**

$$\text{قُلْ إِن كَانَتْ لَكُمُ ٱلدَّارُ ٱلْأَخِرَةُ عِندَ ٱللَّهِ خَالِصَةً مِّن دُونِ ٱلنَّاسِ فَتَمَنَّوُاْ ٱلْمَوْتَ إِن كُنتُمْ صَدِقِينَ ﴿٩٤﴾}$$

94. **Say** (to the Jews to correct their false claims): **"If the Abode of Eternity** [Paradise] **with Allah is exclusive for you, and not the** (other) **people, then wish** (for yourself) **death** (ask for death which will lead you to this good which is intended only for you, and you can reach Paradise quickly), **if you are truthful** (in this claim of yours that Paradise is exclusive for you)!

وَلَن يَتَمَنَّوْهُ أَبَدًا بِمَا قَدَّمَتْ أَيْدِيهِمْ وَٱللَّهُ عَلِيمٌ بِٱلظَّـٰلِمِينَ ﴿٩٥﴾

95. **But they** [the Jews] **will never wish for it** [death] **because** (they fear the punishment of Allah for what) **of what their hands have put forth** [what their hands have sent before them - meaning their evil actions such as disbelief, the rejection and even killing of His prophets, and distortion of His scriptures]. **And Allah knows the oppressors** [that is disbelievers among them and each disbeliever will be punished in the Hereafter because of what they have earned through their evil actions. They knew that their final destination was Hell and this is the reason why they hated death]!

وَلَتَجِدَنَّهُمْ أَحْرَصَ ٱلنَّاسِ عَلَىٰ حَيَوٰةٍ وَمِنَ ٱلَّذِينَ أَشْرَكُواْ يَوَدُّ أَحَدُهُمْ لَوْ يُعَمَّرُ أَلْفَ سَنَةٍ وَمَا هُوَ بِمُزَحْزِحِهِ مِنَ ٱلْعَذَابِ أَن يُعَمَّرَ وَٱللَّهُ بَصِيرٌۢ بِمَا يَعْمَلُونَ ۞

96. **And surely you** (O Prophet) **will find that they** [the Jews] **are the most greedy** (most desirous) **people for life, even** (greedier) **than those who have become polytheists** [those who associate partners with Allah and do not believe in Paradise]; **each of them** [Jews] **would like to be given a life of a thousand years. But his being granted a long life will not remove him from** (eternal) **punishment** (in Hell): **and Allah sees what they do** (this is a threat to them of punishment for their actions)!

قُلْ مَن كَانَ عَدُوًّا لِّـجِبْرِيلَ فَإِنَّهُۥ نَزَّلَهُۥ عَلَىٰ قَلْبِكَ بِإِذْنِ ٱللَّهِ مُصَدِّقًا لِّمَا بَيْنَ يَدَيْهِ وَهُدًى وَبُشْرَىٰ لِلْمُؤْمِنِينَ ۝

97. **Say** (O Prophet) (to the Jews, when they say that Jibril is their enemy, regarding him as bringing down the punishment of Allah): **"Whoever is Jibril's enemy,** (know that) **verily, he** [Jibril] **brought down it** [the Quran] **on your heart with the permission of Allah to confirm the truth of those** [those books of Allah] **that** (were revealed) **before it** [before the Quran], **and as a guide and glad tidings for the believers** (of goodness in this world and in Eternal life).

مَن كَانَ عَدُوًّا لِّلَّهِ وَمَلَـٰٓئِكَتِهِۦ وَرُسُلِهِۦ
وَجِبْرِيلَ وَمِيكَىٰلَ فَإِنَّ ٱللَّهَ عَدُوٌّ
لِّلْكَـٰفِرِينَ ۞ ٩٨

98. **Whoever is an enemy of Allah, and His angels, and His messengers, and** (also two angels) **Jibril, and Mikal** [who even considers an enemy one of those that were listed then he becomes a disbeliever] **then, verily, Allah is the enemy of disbelievers!**

وَلَقَدْ أَنزَلْنَآ إِلَيْكَ ءَايَـٰتٍۭ بَيِّنَـٰتٍ وَمَا
يَكْفُرُ بِهَآ إِلَّا ٱلْفَـٰسِقُونَ ۞ ٩٩

99. **And** (certainly) **indeed We sent down to you** (O Prophet) **clear signs** (by means of which one who seeks guidance will find it and will come to know that

Prophet Muhammad – peace and blessings of Allah be upon him – is the last and final Prophet of Allah), **and no one would deny them** [the clear signs] **except the defiantly disobedient** (those who have abandoned Allah's path – the evildoers who rebel against the command of Allah, refuse to obey Him, and are extremely arrogant).

أَوَ كُلَّمَا عَٰهَدُواْ عَهْدًا نَّبَذَهُۥ فَرِيقٌ مِّنْهُم بَلْ أَكْثَرُهُمْ لَا يُؤْمِنُونَ ﴿١٠٠﴾

100. **Is it not** (true) **that every time they** [the descendants of Israel] **conclude an agreement** (with Allah or people), **some of them** [from the Jews] **reject it** [the agreement] [do not fulfill their agreements]? **But no, most of them do not believe** (in what Allah sent down)!

وَلَمَّا جَآءَهُمْ رَسُولٌ مِّنْ عِندِ ٱللَّهِ مُصَدِّقٌ لِّمَا مَعَهُمْ نَبَذَ فَرِيقٌ مِّنَ ٱلَّذِينَ أُوتُوا۟ ٱلْكِتَٰبَ كِتَٰبَ ٱللَّهِ وَرَآءَ ظُهُورِهِمْ كَأَنَّهُمْ لَا يَعْلَمُونَ ۞ ﴿١٠١﴾

101. **And when a messenger from Allah** [the Prophet Muhammad] **came to them** [to the Jewish priests and scholars], **confirming the truth of the** [Torah] **that is with them** [with the Jews], **some of those to whom the Scripture was given rejected** (threw) **the Scripture of Allah** [Torah] **behind their backs** [did not fulfill the requirements of the Torah on the need to recognize Muhammad, a descendant of the Prophet Ismail, as the Messenger of Allah], **as if they did not know** (these requirements of the Torah).

وَٱتَّبَعُواْ مَا تَتْلُواْ ٱلشَّيَـٰطِينُ عَلَىٰ مُلْكِ سُلَيْمَـٰنَ وَمَا كَفَرَ سُلَيْمَـٰنُ وَلَـٰكِنَّ ٱلشَّيَـٰطِينَ كَفَرُواْ يُعَلِّمُونَ ٱلنَّاسَ ٱلسِّحْرَ وَمَآ أُنزِلَ عَلَى ٱلْمَلَكَيْنِ بِبَابِلَ هَـٰرُوتَ وَمَـٰرُوتَ وَمَا يُعَلِّمَانِ مِنْ أَحَدٍ حَتَّىٰ يَقُولَآ إِنَّمَا نَحْنُ فِتْنَةٌ فَلَا تَكْفُرْ فَيَتَعَلَّمُونَ مِنْهُمَا مَا يُفَرِّقُونَ بِهِۦ بَيْنَ ٱلْمَرْءِ وَزَوْجِهِۦ وَمَا هُم بِضَآرِّينَ بِهِۦ مِنْ

أَحَدٍ إِلَّا بِإِذْنِ ٱللَّهِ وَيَتَعَلَّمُونَ مَا يَضُرُّهُمْ وَلَا يَنفَعُهُمْ وَلَقَدْ عَلِمُوا۟ لَمَنِ ٱشْتَرَىٰهُ مَا لَهُۥ فِى ٱلْءَاخِرَةِ مِنْ خَلَٰقٍ وَلَبِئْسَ مَا شَرَوْا۟ بِهِۦٓ أَنفُسَهُمْ لَوْ كَانُوا۟ يَعْلَمُونَ ﴿١٠٢﴾

102. **And they** [those who rejected the Torah] **followed the** [sorcery] **that the devils read** [recited] **during the reign of** (the prophet) **Suleiman** (peace be upon him). **But Suleiman did not show disbelief and** (did not learn witchcraft), **but nevertheless the shaitans** (themselves) **showed disbelief, teaching people witchcraft. And** (the Jews still followed) **what was sent down** (as a test and a trial from Allah) **to two angels in Babylon,** (whose names were) **Harut and Marut. But they both** [those two angels] **did not teach anyone** (witchcraft) **until they said** (advised them so as to leave no excuse): **"We are only a trial, so**

do not become an unbeliever (by studying witchcraft and obeying the shaitans)!" And (people did not listen to their advice and) learned from them how to separate a husband from his wife. But they [sorcerers] will not be able to harm anyone without the permission of Allah (Magic can only cause harm by Allah's leave, if He wills it). And they [the sorcerers] were trained in that which harmed them (themselves) and did not benefit them. And (certainly) they [the Jews] knew that the one who acquired this [witchcraft] - (then) there is no share (good) for him in Eternal life (the Hereafter). And how bad (wretched) is that [witchcraft and unbelief] what they sold their souls for - if only they knew! (They preferred the life of this world to the Hereafter)

وَلَوۡ أَنَّهُمۡ ءَامَنُواْ وَٱتَّقَوۡاْ لَمَثُوبَةٌ مِّنۡ عِندِ ٱللَّهِ خَيۡرٌ لَّوۡ كَانُواْ يَعۡلَمُونَ ﴿١٠٣﴾

103. **And if they** [the Jews] **would believe** (verily) **and would beware** (feared the punishment of Allah - by fulfilling His commands and avoiding what He forbade), **then the reward** (for this) **from Allah** (would be for them) **better** (than what they have chosen for themselves) - **if** (only) **they knew!**

يَـٰٓأَيُّهَا ٱلَّذِينَ ءَامَنُوا۟ لَا تَقُولُوا۟ رَٰعِنَا وَقُولُوا۟ ٱنظُرْنَا وَٱسْمَعُوا۟ وَلِلْكَـٰفِرِينَ عَذَابٌ أَلِيمٌ ﴿١٠٤﴾

104. **O those who believe! Do not say** (to the Messenger of Allah) (when addressing him with a speech): "(*Ra'ina*) **Pay attention to us!**" (The Jews used to say this Arabic word with bad intentions, and said it intending its meaning in Hebrew which denotes an insult) - **and** (to prevent mockery you should instead) **say:** "(*Un'zurna*) **Make us understand!**" -

and listen (to the Quran, Sunnah, and what you are commanded and do it). **And for the unbelievers** (who mock the Messenger of Allah) - **a painful punishment!**

مَّا يَوَدُّ ٱلَّذِينَ كَفَرُواْ مِنْ أَهْلِ ٱلْكِتَـٰبِ وَلَا ٱلْمُشْرِكِينَ أَن يُنَزَّلَ عَلَيْكُم مِّنْ خَيْرٍ مِّن رَّبِّكُمْ وَٱللَّهُ يَخْتَصُّ بِرَحْمَتِهِۦ مَن يَشَآءُ وَٱللَّهُ ذُو ٱلْفَضْلِ ٱلْعَظِيمِ ﴿١٠٥﴾

105. **Those who became unbelievers,** (neither) **from** (among) **the people of the Scripture and nor** (from among) **the polytheists,** (because of their envy and hatred) **would not want to be sent down to you** (O believers) (any) **goodness from your Lord** (in the form of revelation, useful knowledge, help or good news). **But Allah chooses for His mercy whom He wills, for Allah is the**

possessor [giver] of great bounty! (It is from Allah's bounty that He sent His Prophet – peace and blessings of Allah be upon him – and revealed His scripture to us.)

﴿ ۞ مَا نَنسَخْ مِنْ ءَايَةٍ أَوْ نُنسِهَا نَأْتِ بِخَيْرٍ مِّنْهَآ أَوْ مِثْلِهَآ أَلَمْ تَعْلَمْ أَنَّ ٱللَّهَ عَلَىٰ كُلِّ شَىْءٍ قَدِيرٌ ١٠٦ ﴾

106. **If We** [Allah] **abrogate** (any) *ayat* (verse from the Quran) **or cause to be forgotten, then we give a better one than it** [more beneficial than this verse], **or equal to it.** (Such instances occur because of Allah's wisdom, mercy, and knowledge. He does as He wishes and whatever He does is in the best interests of His servants even though they may not realize it.) **Do you not know that Allah is powerful over everything?** (Allah is able to do all things.)

أَلَمْ تَعْلَمْ أَنَّ ٱللَّهَ لَهُۥ مُلْكُ ٱلسَّمَـٰوَٰتِ وَٱلْأَرْضِ ۗ وَمَا لَكُم مِّن دُونِ ٱللَّهِ مِن وَلِيٍّ وَلَا نَصِيرٍ ﴿١٠٧﴾

107. **Did you not know that Allah** (is such that) **to Him** (belongs) (all) **power over the heavens and the earth?** (Everything belongs to Allah, and He completely controls everything, and every, even the smallest, event occurs only according to His knowledge and according to His will. He does what He wants, Rules what He wants, commands His servants and forbids them as He wants, and they must obey and accept.) (And let those who disobey Allah know that) **you have, besides Allah, no protector** (who would intercede for you), **nor a helper** (who would protect you from the punishment of Allah).

أَمْ تُرِيدُونَ أَن تَسْـَٔلُوا۟ رَسُولَكُمْ كَمَا سُئِلَ مُوسَىٰ مِن قَبْلُ ۗ وَمَن يَتَبَدَّلِ ٱلْكُفْرَ بِٱلْإِيمَٰنِ فَقَدْ ضَلَّ سَوَآءَ ٱلسَّبِيلِ ﴿١٠٨﴾

108. **Or do you** (O people) **want to ask your messenger** [Prophet Muhammad – peace and blessings of Allah be upon him] [to ask him unnecessary questions persistently with the intent of stubbornness and arrogance, and ask him for miracles], (in the same way) **as** (the descendants of Israel) **asked Musa before? And** (know that if) **whoever replaces faith with unbelief** [becomes an unbeliever], **he has already gone astray** [fell into error and away from the straight path into ignorance and misguidance].

وَدَّ كَثِيرٌ مِّنْ أَهْلِ ٱلْكِتَٰبِ لَوْ يَرُدُّونَكُم مِّنۢ بَعْدِ إِيمَٰنِكُمْ كُفَّارًا حَسَدًا مِّنْ عِندِ أَنفُسِهِم مِّنۢ بَعْدِ مَا تَبَيَّنَ لَهُمُ ٱلْحَقُّ فَٱعْفُوا۟ وَٱصْفَحُوا۟ حَتَّىٰ يَأْتِىَ ٱللَّهُ بِأَمْرِهِۦٓ إِنَّ ٱللَّهَ عَلَىٰ كُلِّ شَىْءٍ قَدِيرٌ ﴿١٠٩﴾

109. **Many of the People of the Book would like to convert you after your belief to unbelievers** (turn you back to disbelief that is the worship of idols and graves) **out of envy from themselves** [since Faith is the greatest good that Allah gives in this world], (even) **after the truth became clear to them** [the People of the Book that Muhammad – peace and blessings of Allah be upon him – is Allah's final Prophet]. **But** (you believers) **excuse** [do not reproach them for this – pardon them] **and turn away** (from them) **until Allah comes with** (another

of) **His command** [with the command to fight them]. **Verily, Allah is powerful over everything!**

وَأَقِيمُوا۟ ٱلصَّلَوٰةَ وَءَاتُوا۟ ٱلزَّكَوٰةَ وَمَا تُقَدِّمُوا۟ لِأَنفُسِكُم مِّنْ خَيْرٍ تَجِدُوهُ عِندَ ٱللَّهِ إِنَّ ٱللَّهَ بِمَا تَعْمَلُونَ بَصِيرٌ ۝

110. **And** (make the most of your present time on earth and) **pray** (duly perform *As-Salah* – the prayer – and establish it with all its parts, both obligatory and recommended aspects) **and give obligatory alms** [*zakat*] (to those who are entitled to it); **and what you prepare for yourselves from good** [righteous deeds and property spent for the sake of Allah], **you will find it with Allah** [on the Day of Judgment and the reward for these good actions will be Paradise in the Eternal Life]: **verily, Allah sees what you do!** (He sees all that you do and will reward you for them.)

وَقَالُواْ لَن يَدْخُلَ ٱلْجَنَّةَ إِلَّا مَن كَانَ هُودًا أَوْ نَصَٰرَىٰ ۗ تِلْكَ أَمَانِيُّهُمْ ۗ قُلْ هَاتُواْ بُرْهَٰنَكُمْ إِن كُنتُمْ صَٰدِقِينَ ﴿١١١﴾

111. **And they** [Jews and Christians] **say:** **"No one will enter Paradise except those who are Jews or Christians."** These are their wishful thinking (their own vain desires). **Say** (O Prophet – peace and blessings of Allah be upon him): **"Provide your evidence if you are truthful** (in your statements)!"

بَلَىٰ مَنْ أَسْلَمَ وَجْهَهُۥ لِلَّهِ وَهُوَ مُحْسِنٌ فَلَهُۥٓ أَجْرُهُۥ عِندَ رَبِّهِۦ وَلَا خَوْفٌ عَلَيْهِمْ وَلَا هُمْ يَحْزَنُونَ ﴿١١٢﴾

112. But no! Whoever surrenders his face to Allah [who completely submits to Allah – becomes a Muslim], **while being a doer of good** (*Muhsin* – that is a good-doer who does good actions for Allah's sake only without any show off or to gain praise or fame, etc., and in accordance with the *Sunnah* of Allah's Messenger Muhammad – peace and blessings of Allah be upon him), **then he** (will be given) **his reward with his Lord** (Paradise in Eternal Life), **and there will be no fear over them** (before what awaits them in Eternal Life), **and they will not grieve** (due to parting with worldly goods, that is they will not grieve for what they have missed from the fortunes of this world).

وَقَالَتِ ٱلْيَهُودُ لَيْسَتِ ٱلنَّصَرَىٰ عَلَىٰ شَيْءٍ

وَقَالَتِ ٱلنَّصَرَىٰ لَيْسَتِ ٱلْيَهُودُ عَلَىٰ شَيْءٍ

وَهُمْ يَتْلُونَ ٱلْكِتَٰبَ كَذَٰلِكَ قَالَ ٱلَّذِينَ لَا

يَعْلَمُونَ مِثْلَ قَوْلِهِمْ فَٱللَّهُ يَحْكُمُ بَيْنَهُمْ

يَوْمَ ٱلْقِيَـٰمَةِ فِيمَا كَانُوا فِيهِ يَخْتَلِفُونَ ﴿١١٣﴾

113. **And the Jews said: "Christians are on nothing** [not on the truth]!**" And the Christians said: "Jews are on nothing!" And** (this is at the same time when) **they read the Scripture** [Torah and Gospel] (which contains the command to believe in all the prophets). **So** (also) **say those who do not know** [those who have not read the scriptures – the polytheists pagans], **similar to their words** [the words of the People of the Book]. **Allah will judge between them on the Day of Resurrection regarding what they differed** (in opinion).

وَمَنْ أَظْلَمُ مِمَّن مَّنَعَ مَسَٰجِدَ ٱللَّهِ أَن يُذْكَرَ فِيهَا ٱسْمُهُۥ وَسَعَىٰ فِى خَرَابِهَآ أُوْلَٰٓئِكَ مَا كَانَ لَهُمْ أَن يَدْخُلُوهَآ إِلَّا خَآئِفِينَ لَهُمْ فِى ٱلدُّنْيَا خِزْىٌ وَلَهُمْ فِى ٱلْأَخِرَةِ عَذَابٌ عَظِيمٌ ۝

114. **And who are more oppressive than those who prevent the remembrance of Allah's name in the mosques of Allah** [preventing prayers and recitation of the Book of Allah in the mosques] **and seek to destroy them** (destroying, closing or preventing the believers from entering them)? **Those** [such] **should only enter there** (Allah's mosques) **being afraid** (that they will be punished for this). **For them in** (this) **world is a disgrace** (shame and humiliation), **and for them in Eternal life is a great punishment!**

وَلِلَّهِ ٱلْمَشْرِقُ وَٱلْمَغْرِبُ فَأَيْنَمَا تُوَلُّواْ فَثَمَّ وَجْهُ ٱللَّهِ إِنَّ ٱللَّهَ وَٰسِعٌ عَلِيمٌ ۝

115. **And** (only) **to Allah belongs both the east and the west** (and what is between them) [Allah is the Lord and Ruler of everything]; **and wherever you turn** [turned], **then there** [in that direction] **is the** (Honorable and Noble) **Face of Allah** (and He is High above, over His Throne). **Verily, Allah is all-Encompassing** (with His knowledge, power, vision) (and) **Knowing** (everything)**!**

وَقَالُواْ ٱتَّخَذَ ٱللَّهُ وَلَدًا سُبْحَٰنَهُۥ بَل لَّهُۥ مَا فِى ٱلسَّمَٰوَٰتِ وَٱلْأَرْضِ كُلٌّ لَّهُۥ قَٰنِتُونَ ۝

116. **And they** [the disbelievers] **said: "Allah has taken a child for Himself** (begotten a son)." [The Jews said that Uzayr is the son of Allah; Christians said

that Jesus is the son of Allah; and the polytheists said that the angels are the daughters of Allah.] **Glorified is He** [Exalted be He above all that they associate with Him. It is not befitting to His Majesty to have children]! [If He had a child, then he would have to be like Him, and there is nothing like Him.] **On the contrary**, (He does not need anyone and has no need for His creation) [He does not have any flaws] (and) **He owns everything** (to Him belongs all) **that is in the heavens and on earth! All devoutly obey** (surrender with obedience in worship to) **Him** (because they are in His possession and under His control)!

بَدِيعُ ٱلسَّمَـٰوَٰتِ وَٱلْأَرْضِ ۖ وَإِذَا قَضَىٰٓ أَمْرًا فَإِنَّمَا يَقُولُ لَهُۥ كُن فَيَكُونُ ﴿١١٧﴾

117. (Allah) **is the Originator of the heavens and the earth** (Who created them in a perfect matter without any precedent or prototype), **and when He**

decrees (and wills) **a matter** (decides to do anything) **then He only says to it** (once): **"Be!"** - **and it** (immediately) **happens** [occurs]. (Nothing can stop Allah's command and His decree.)

$$\text{وَقَالَ ٱلَّذِينَ لَا يَعْلَمُونَ لَوْلَا يُكَلِّمُنَا ٱللَّهُ أَوْ تَأْتِينَا ءَايَةٌ ۗ كَذَٰلِكَ قَالَ ٱلَّذِينَ مِن قَبْلِهِم مِّثْلَ قَوْلِهِمْ ۘ تَشَٰبَهَتْ قُلُوبُهُمْ ۗ قَدْ بَيَّنَّا ٱلْءَايَٰتِ لِقَوْمٍ يُوقِنُونَ ۝١١٨}$$

118. **And those who know nothing** (from among the People of the Scripture and the idolaters about the purpose of the coming of the Prophets) **said** (in their stubbornness against the truth): **"If Allah spoke to us** (and said that this person is in fact His messenger) **or if a sign came to us** (about that he is indeed the Messenger of Allah)!" (They do not say this because they want the truth, but only because of their

stubbornness, since Allah has always given His messengers sufficient signs to prove the truth that they are messengers.) **So also said those who were before them** (in the past) (to the former Prophets) **like their words; the hearts of them** [both the former and these unbelievers] **are similar** (because all disbelievers are the same in the way they reject the truth even if they are from different places and times). **We have already made clear the signs** (proofs) **for the people who are convinced** [for those who have faith].

إِنَّآ أَرْسَلْنَٰكَ بِٱلْحَقِّ بَشِيرًا وَنَذِيرًا وَلَا تُسْـَٔلُ عَنْ أَصْحَٰبِ ٱلْجَحِيمِ ﴿١١٩﴾

119. **Indeed, We sent you** (O Muhammad – peace and blessings of Allah be upon him) **with the truth** [with the Book of Allah and His Law] (to all people) **as a bearer of glad tidings** (rejoicing the believers with Paradise) **and a warner** (warning those who

persist in disbelief with punishment in Hell), **and you** (O Muhammad) (after bringing the truth to them – your responsibility is only to convey the message) **you will not be asked** [you will not be responsible] **about the inhabitants of the fire** [Hell].

وَلَن تَرْضَىٰ عَنكَ ٱلْيَهُودُ وَلَا ٱلنَّصَرَىٰ حَتَّىٰ تَتَّبِعَ مِلَّتَهُمْ قُلْ إِنَّ هُدَى ٱللَّهِ هُوَ ٱلْهُدَىٰ وَلَئِنِ ٱتَّبَعْتَ أَهْوَآءَهُم بَعْدَ ٱلَّذِى جَآءَكَ مِنَ ٱلْعِلْمِ مَا لَكَ مِنَ ٱللَّهِ مِن وَلِىٍّ وَلَا نَصِيرٍ ۝

120. Neither Jews nor Christians will ever be pleased with you until you follow their beliefs [the faith of each, respectively]. **Say: "Indeed, (only) the guidance of Allah is the** (true) **guidance** (and not the one on which each of you are)!" **And if you** (O

Prophet) (though this verse is addressed specifically to the Prophet – peace and blessings of Allah be upon him – it is addressed to the Muslims in general) **follow their desires after what has come to you** (by revelation) **from knowledge** (the clear truth – the Quran and the Sunnah), **then there will be neither a protector nor a helper for you against Allah.** (This verse contains a stern warning to the Muslims against following or imitating the Jews and Christians)

ٱلَّذِينَ ءَاتَيْنَـٰهُمُ ٱلْكِتَـٰبَ يَتْلُونَهُۥ حَقَّ تِلَاوَتِهِۦٓ أُو۟لَـٰٓئِكَ يُؤْمِنُونَ بِهِۦ ۗ وَمَن يَكْفُرْ بِهِۦ فَأُو۟لَـٰٓئِكَ هُمُ ٱلْخَـٰسِرُونَ ﴿١٢١﴾

121. **Those to whom We have given the Scripture** [the people of this community and previous ones] (and who) **recite it** [the Scripture given to them] **as it should be recited** (that is as it

should be followed by obeying its orders and following its teachings. They do not change it. They consider its permitted as permitted, and consider its forbidden as forbidden. When heaven is mentioned in the Quran, they ask for heaven and when hell is mentioned, they seek refuge from it), **they** (are the ones who) **believe in it. And whoever shows disbelief in it** [in the Scriptures], **then those** [such] – **are the losers.** (This verse clarifies that the right of reciting the Quran is that it should be acted upon.)

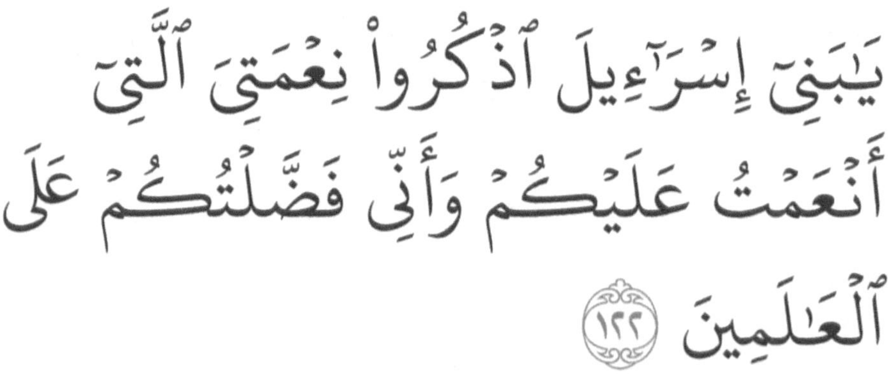

122. O Children of Israel! Remember My favor which I have bestowed upon you, (and remember) that I gave you preference over (those) worlds [favored you over

the people who lived in your time] (prophets were sent to you and books from Allah were sent down to you).

وَٱتَّقُواْ يَوْمًا لَّا تَجْزِى نَفْسٌ عَن نَّفْسٍ شَيْئًا وَلَا يُقْبَلُ مِنْهَا عَدْلٌ وَلَا تَنفَعُهَا شَفَٰعَةٌ وَلَا هُمْ يُنصَرُونَ ﴿١٢٣﴾

123. **And beware of the Day** [fear the horrors of the Day of Judgment] (protect yourself by following the instructions of Allah and keeping away from what He has prohibited), **when** (one) **soul will not repay for** (another) **soul** [no soul will be able to help another soul in any way], **and compensation** [ransom] **will not be accepted from it** (no matter how great), **and no intercession will bring it benefit** (no one pleading on its behalf will benefit it, no matter how high their position, if he did not believe during his life on earth), **and they will not be helped** (in salvation

from the punishment of Allah)! (Other than Allah a soul will have no helper on the Day of Judgment.)

۞ وَإِذِ ٱبْتَلَىٰٓ إِبْرَٰهِـۧمَ رَبُّهُۥ بِكَلِمَـٰتٍ فَأَتَمَّهُنَّ ۖ قَالَ إِنِّى جَاعِلُكَ لِلنَّاسِ إِمَامًا ۖ قَالَ وَمِن ذُرِّيَّتِى ۖ قَالَ لَا يَنَالُ عَهْدِى ٱلظَّـٰلِمِينَ ﴿١٢٤﴾

124. **And** (remember) **when Ibrahim was tested by the Lord with** (certain) **Words** [commands], **and he** [Ibrahim] **completely fulfilled them** (perfectly). **He** (Allah) **said: "Indeed, I will make you** (Ibrahim) **for the people** (who will be after you) **a leader** [example]." **He** [Ibrahim] **said: "And from my offspring?"** (Ibrahim asked Allah to make all his descendants also leaders who people would be guided by and a good example.) **He** (Allah) **said: "My covenant** [My promise to you about this] **will not**

reach the wrongdoers (from your offspring) [the unbelievers will not be included in this promise and it will only be bestowed upon the righteous people among his descendants who submitted themselves to Allah.]."

وَإِذْ جَعَلْنَا ٱلْبَيْتَ مَثَابَةً لِّلنَّاسِ وَأَمْنًا وَٱتَّخِذُواْ مِن مَّقَامِ إِبْرَاهِـۧمَ مُصَلًّى وَعَهِدْنَا إِلَىٰ إِبْرَاهِـۧمَ وَإِسْمَـٰعِيلَ أَن طَهِّرَا بَيْتِيَ لِلطَّآئِفِينَ وَٱلْعَـٰكِفِينَ وَٱلرُّكَّعِ ٱلسُّجُودِ ۝١٢٥

125. **And** (remember) **when We made this house** [Kaaba] **a place of return** (where they return to make pilgrimages and which they remember before each prayer when they take prayer direction) **for people and a place of safety** (where people are safe for themselves and for their property): "**And take** (O believers) **for yourself from the place of**

Ibrahim [The place of standing of Ibrahim is a stone with footprints of the Prophet Ibrahim, peace be upon him, on which he stood during the construction of the Kaaba. Near this place, the pilgrim prays after circumambulating the Kaaba] **a place to pray." And We commanded Ibrahim and Ismail: "Cleanse My house** [Kaaba] (from filth) **for those who circumambulate** (around it), **and stay** (there for the purpose of worshiping Allah), **and bow down** [perform bows to Allah] **and prostrate!"**

وَإِذْ قَالَ إِبْرَٰهِـۧمُ رَبِّ ٱجْعَلْ هَـٰذَا بَلَدًا ءَامِنًا وَٱرْزُقْ أَهْلَهُۥ مِنَ ٱلثَّمَرَٰتِ مَنْ ءَامَنَ مِنْهُم بِٱللَّهِ وَٱلْيَوْمِ ٱلْأَخِرِ قَالَ وَمَن كَفَرَ فَأُمَتِّعُهُۥ قَلِيلًا ثُمَّ أَضْطَرُّهُۥٓ إِلَىٰ عَذَابِ ٱلنَّارِ وَبِئْسَ ٱلْمَصِيرُ ﴿١٢٦﴾

126. **And** (mention that) **as Ibrahim said: "Lord! Make this** [Makkah] **a safe city and give its inhabitants produce** (fruits, crops), **those of them who believe in Allah and the Last Day.** [The Day of Judgment is also called the Last Day, since after this day there are no more days.]" (Allah accepted his prayer and) **said: "And to those who became disbelievers, I** (also) **will give a little** (and not for long) **enjoyment** (by giving them provision in this life), **and then I will force them to the punishment of Fire** (in the next life)." **And** (how) **awful** (wretched) **it** (Hell) **is a return place** (their final destination to which they return on the Day of Judgment)!

وَإِذْ يَرْفَعُ إِبْرَٰهِـۧمُ ٱلْقَوَاعِدَ مِنَ ٱلْبَيْتِ وَإِسْمَٰعِيلُ رَبَّنَا تَقَبَّلْ مِنَّآ إِنَّكَ أَنتَ ٱلسَّمِيعُ ٱلْعَلِيمُ ﴿١٢٧﴾

127. **And** (mention about) **how** (the Prophet) **Ibrahim was raising the foundations of the house** [Kaaba – how they did this great task fearing and hoping from Allah], **and** (with him his son) **Ismail** (assisting him). (And each of them turned with a prayer to Allah): "(O) **our Lord! Accept** (all we did including building the Kaaba, and accept our supplications. They were raising the foundations of House of Allah yet they were afraid that Allah will not accept it from them. This is how believers are. They do good actions fearing that their good deeds may not be accepted of them.) **from us**, (for) **truly, You are the Ever-Hearing, the Ever-Knowing** (of our intentions and everything that we do)!"

رَبَّنَا وَٱجْعَلْنَا مُسْلِمَيْنِ لَكَ وَمِن ذُرِّيَّتِنَآ أُمَّةً مُّسْلِمَةً لَّكَ وَأَرِنَا مَنَاسِكَنَا وَتُبْ عَلَيْنَآ إِنَّكَ أَنتَ ٱلتَّوَّابُ ٱلرَّحِيمُ ﴿١٢٨﴾

128. (They continued to pray to Allah) "(O) **Our Lord! And make us** (both) **Muslims** (in submission) **to You** (they prayed to Allah to make them surrender in devotion to His command, to be humble towards Him, and not worshipping anyone besides Him) and from our offspring – a Muslim nation (in submission) **to You** (the community that surrendered to Allah, which the Prophets Ibrahim and Ismail asked for, is the community of the prophet Muhammad. This is because Prophet Muhammad is a descendant of these Prophets: Ibrahim and Ismail), **and show us** [explain] **the rites of our worship** (teach us how to worship You), **and accept our repentance** (to forgive them for their faults and shortcomings in doing what He instructed them), (for) **verily, You are the Accepting of Repentance, the Merciful!"**

رَّبَّنَا وَٱبْعَثْ فِيهِمْ رَسُولًا مِّنْهُمْ يَتْلُوا۟ عَلَيْهِمْ ءَايَٰتِكَ وَيُعَلِّمُهُمُ ٱلْكِتَٰبَ وَٱلْحِكْمَةَ وَيُزَكِّيهِمْ ۚ إِنَّكَ أَنتَ ٱلْعَزِيزُ ٱلْحَكِيمُ ﴿١٢٩﴾

129. "(O) **Our Lord! And send forth** [choose] **among them** (from the descendants of Ismail) **a Messenger,** (one) **of them** (and Allah answered their invocation by sending Muhammad – peace and blessings of Allah be upon him), **who will recite to them Your signs** (*ayats*, verses), **and teach them the Scripture** [Quran] **and** (the) **wisdom** [Sunnah and the features of the law of Allah], **and cleanse them** (from worshipping others alongside Allah, that is the filth of polytheism, and purify them from all evil actions), (for) **truly, You are the Ever-Mighty, the Ever-Wise** (in what You does and in Your decrees)!"

وَمَن يَرْغَبُ عَن مِّلَّةِ إِبْرَٰهِـۧمَ إِلَّا مَن سَفِهَ نَفْسَهُۥ وَلَقَدِ ٱصْطَفَيْنَٰهُ فِى ٱلدُّنْيَا وَإِنَّهُۥ فِى ٱلْءَاخِرَةِ لَمِنَ ٱلصَّٰلِحِينَ ﴿١٣٠﴾

130. **And who will turn away from the religion of Ibrahim** [who will leave monotheism and worshipping only Allah; that is who will leave Islam], **except** (only) **the one who has made his soul stupid** (that is only a fool will turn away)? (Similarly only a wise person follows the religion of Ibrahim which is Islam). **And** (certainly) **We chose him in** (this) **world** (making high his position among the messengers), **and, verily, he in Eternal life** (in the Hereafter) **will be certainly among the righteous.** (He fulfilled what Allah commanded him to do, and so reached the highest levels.)

إِذْ قَالَ لَهُۥ رَبُّهُۥٓ أَسْلِمْ قَالَ أَسْلَمْتُ لِرَبِّ
ٱلْعَـٰلَمِينَ ﴿١٣١﴾

131. (Remember) **how his Lord said to him** [Ibrahim]: **"Submit** [be a monotheist, that is a Muslim and completely submit to Allah]!" **He said: "I have submitted** (in Islam with sincerity, affirming Allah's Oneness, out of love for Him, and repentance) **to the Lord of the worlds!"** (*Tawheed* – worshipping only Allah became the defining characteristic of Ibrahim. He rushed to Islam without any hesitation.)

وَوَصَّىٰ بِهَآ إِبْرَٰهِـۧمُ بَنِيهِ وَيَعْقُوبُ يَـٰبَنِىَّ
إِنَّ ٱللَّهَ ٱصْطَفَىٰ لَكُمُ ٱلدِّينَ فَلَا تَمُوتُنَّ
إِلَّا وَأَنتُم مُّسْلِمُونَ ﴿١٣٢﴾

132. **And enjoined this Ibrahim to his sons** [to say and follow the words "I surrendered to the Lord of the worlds!"] **and** (also) **Yaqoob** (saying): **"O my sons! Indeed, Allah has chosen for you** (out of mercy and kindness) **the belief** [monotheism and obedience to Allah, that is Islam]; **therefore, do not die in any other way, except** (while) **you are Muslims** [always be believers in Allah and obey His commands]!"

أَمْ كُنتُمْ شُهَدَآءَ إِذْ حَضَرَ يَعْقُوبَ ٱلْمَوْتُ إِذْ قَالَ لِبَنِيهِ مَا تَعْبُدُونَ مِنْ بَعْدِى قَالُوا۟ نَعْبُدُ إِلَٰهَكَ وَإِلَٰهَ ءَابَآئِكَ إِبْرَٰهِۦمَ وَإِسْمَٰعِيلَ وَإِسْحَٰقَ إِلَٰهًا وَٰحِدًا وَنَحْنُ لَهُۥ مُسْلِمُونَ ۝١٣٣

133. **Or were you** (Jews of Madinah) **witnesses** [were present] **when death came** [approached] **to Yaqoob**, (and) **when he said to his sons** [Yusuf and his brothers]: **"What will you worship after me** [after my death]?" **They said: "We will worship your God and the God of your fathers - Ibrahim, and Ismail, and Ishaq - the Only** (true One) **God, and to Him we are Muslims** [obey and humble ourselves to His command, that is submit to Him in Islam]."

تِلْكَ أُمَّةٌ قَدْ خَلَتْ لَهَا مَا كَسَبَتْ وَلَكُم مَّا كَسَبْتُمْ وَلَا تُسْـَٔلُونَ عَمَّا كَانُوا۟ يَعْمَلُونَ ﴿١٣٤﴾

134. **That** (nation) [the prophets Ibrahim and Yaqoob with their sons] **is a nation that has already passed** [which is no longer there]; **to it** (that nation) **- what it has earned** [earning either good or evil, and you will not be credited with anything from their deeds], **and to you what you have earned** [they

will not gain anything from your deeds], **and you will not be asked about what they did.** (No one is held responsible for the disobedience and sins of another, but everyone is rewarded according to their own deeds. Only your good actions will benefit you.)

وَقَالُواْ كُونُواْ هُودًا أَوْ نَصَـٰرَىٰ تَهْتَدُواْ قُلْ بَلْ مِلَّةَ إِبْرَٰهِـٰمَ حَنِيفًا وَمَا كَانَ مِنَ ٱلْمُشْرِكِينَ ﴿١٣٥﴾

135. **And they said** [Jews and Christians] (to Muslims): **"Become Jews or Nasara** (Christians) - (and then you) (will be guided) **on the right path** [on the truth]." **Say** (to them): "**No,** (rather let us all follow) **the creed** [faith] (of Prophet) **Ibrahim,** (who was) *Hanif* [monotheist, turning away from idolatry and worshipping none but Allah alone], **and he was not from** (among) **the polytheists** (those who associate others with Allah)."

قُولُوٓاْ ءَامَنَّا بِٱللَّهِ وَمَآ أُنزِلَ إِلَيْنَا وَمَآ أُنزِلَ إِلَىٰٓ إِبْرَٰهِـۧمَ وَإِسْمَٰعِيلَ وَإِسْحَٰقَ وَيَعْقُوبَ وَٱلْأَسْبَاطِ وَمَآ أُوتِىَ مُوسَىٰ وَعِيسَىٰ وَمَآ أُوتِىَ ٱلنَّبِيُّونَ مِن رَّبِّهِمْ لَا نُفَرِّقُ بَيْنَ أَحَدٍ مِّنْهُمْ وَنَحْنُ لَهُۥ مُسْلِمُونَ ﴿١٣٦﴾

136. **Say** (O believers, that is Muslims, announce your beliefs openly and call people to it): **"We** (the believers are like a single body, and Muslims should therefore be united and their call should be one) **believed in Allah** (in Islam and we do the righteous actions of a Muslim. Belief in the heart is reflected in words and deeds) **and in what was sent down to us** [the Quran], **and what was sent down to Ibrahim** [ten scrolls], **Ismail, Ishaq, Yaqoob and the descendants** [Prophets from the twelve generations

of the descendants of the Prophet Yaqoob], **and what was given to Musa** [Torah] **and Jesus** [Gospel], **and what was given to the Prophets from their Lord** [the former Scriptures]. **We do not distinguish between any of them** (we don't have faith in some and reject others like the Jews and Christians), **and we surrender to Him** (Allah as Muslims in Islam)."

فَإِنْ ءَامَنُواْ بِمِثْلِ مَآ ءَامَنتُم بِهِۦ فَقَدِ ٱهْتَدَواْ وَّإِن تَوَلَّوْاْ فَإِنَّمَا هُمْ فِى شِقَاقٍ فَسَيَكْفِيكَهُمُ ٱللَّهُ وَهُوَ ٱلسَّمِيعُ ٱلْعَلِيمُ ۝١٣٧

137. **If they** [disbelievers] **believe in something similar to what you** (O believers) **believed** [that the Quran is from Allah and Muhammad is His Messenger], **then they will indeed be on the** (true) **path; and if they turn away** (if they reject the truth, that is all the prophets or some of them) **then they**

(are) **in opposition** [are against you and are in disagreement and mutual contradiction]. **And Allah will deliver you** (O Messenger) **from them** [from their evil] (and He will help you and give you victory over them), **for He is the Ever-Hearing, the Ever-Knowing** (knows all their intentions and actions).

صِبْغَةَ ٱللَّهِ وَمَنْ أَحْسَنُ مِنَ ٱللَّهِ صِبْغَةً وَنَحْنُ لَهُۥ عَٰبِدُونَ ﴿١٣٨﴾

138. (And say, "Ours is) **coloring** [faith or religion] **of Allah** [complete obedience to Allah - Islam]! **And who can give a better color** (faith or religion**) than Allah? And we** (only) **worship Him** (sincerely by following the Quran and Sunnah). (A person should color himself in the color of Allah, that is he should submit himself entirely to the Will of Allah, which is possible only after accepting His Guidance and believing in all His Prophets. There is no color that is worse or uglier than a person who colors himself with

something other than the color given by Allah, that is follows a religion other than His.)

قُلْ أَتُحَآجُّونَنَا فِى ٱللَّهِ وَهُوَ رَبُّنَا وَرَبُّكُمْ وَلَنَآ أَعْمَٰلُنَا وَلَكُمْ أَعْمَٰلُكُمْ وَنَحْنُ لَهُۥ مُخْلِصُونَ ﴿١٣٩﴾

139. **Say** (to the People of the Book): **"Are you arguing with us about Allah, while He is our Lord and your Lord?** (The claim of the People of the Book – the Jews and Christians – that they are closer to Allah is not true. Allah does not belong to any single race or community. Only a person who is sincere to Allah alone in his righteous actions is closer to Allah.) **And to us - our deeds** [Allah will not ask us about your deeds], **and to you - your deeds** [and you will not be asked about our deeds], (each person will be rewarded according to what he has done), **and we are sincere** [in deed and intention] **to Him."**

أَمۡ تَقُولُونَ إِنَّ إِبۡرَٰهِۦمَ وَإِسۡمَٰعِيلَ وَإِسۡحَٰقَ وَيَعۡقُوبَ وَٱلۡأَسۡبَاطَ كَانُواْ هُودًا أَوۡ نَصَٰرَىٰ قُلۡ ءَأَنتُمۡ أَعۡلَمُ أَمِ ٱللَّهُ وَمَنۡ أَظۡلَمُ مِمَّن كَتَمَ شَهَٰدَةً عِندَهُۥ مِنَ ٱللَّهِ وَمَا ٱللَّهُ بِغَٰفِلٍ عَمَّا تَعۡمَلُونَ ﴿١٤٠﴾

140. **Or will you** (O People of the Book) **say that Ibrahim, and Ismail, and Ishaq, and Yakub, and the tribes** [the prophets who were in the twelve generations of the descendants of Israel] **were Jews or Christians? Say: "Do you know more or Allah** (knows better that they all were Muslims)**? And who** (is) **more oppressive than the one who hid in himself the evidence** (which he had) **from Allah** (that is to believe in Prophet Muhammad – peace and blessings of Allah be upon him when he

comes, as is written in their Books)? **And Allah is not unaware about what you do** (and you will be rewarded accordingly. This is a threat and a warning to them.)!"

تِلْكَ أُمَّةٌ قَدْ خَلَتْ ۖ لَهَا مَا كَسَبَتْ وَلَكُم مَّا كَسَبْتُمْ ۖ وَلَا تُسْـَٔلُونَ عَمَّا كَانُوا يَعْمَلُونَ ﴿١٤١﴾

141. **That** (community) [Ibrahim with his sons and Yaqoob with his sons] **is a community that has already passed on; to it** [that community] - **what it has gained** [you will not be credited with anything from their deeds], **and to you what you have gained** [they will not gain anything from your deeds], **and you will not be asked about what they did.** (No one is held accountable for another's disobedience and sin, and no one benefits from another's good righteous actions. Each person will receive his reward, depending on what they themselves do.)